AF370504

The Mind-Boggling Encyclopedia of

Famous People´s
Last Words
Before Dying

ESPEN F. KJENDLIE

Encyclopedia Publishing House
encyclopediapublishing.com

The Mind-Boggling Encyclopedia of Famous People´s Last Words Before Dying

Author: Espen F. Kjendlie espen@encyclopediapublishing.com

Publisher: Encyclopedia Publishing House

More information: www.encyclopediapublishing.com.

Contact: editor@encyclopediapublishing.com

Publication Information: This book was published by Encyclopedia Publishing House in 2023 and is printed on 50lb Creme paper.

Typography and Editing: The text of this book is set in Minion Pro Regular 10 for the body text and Minion Pro 14 for headings and subheadings. The typography was designed to ensure readability and visual appeal. The text of this book was edited for accuracy, clarity, and consistency. The satirical tone and humorous language were carefully crafted to highlight the stupidity of war while maintaining a respectful and informative approach.

ISBN: 978-82-693278-4-7

Cover Design: The cover design was created by Espen F. Kjendlie. Cover on edvard munch´s painting "The Scream" (1893). Vectors by Vecteezy.com.

Disclaimer: The views and opinions expressed in this book are those of the author and do not necessarily reflect the views of the publisher or any other parties mentioned.

acknowledgements: The purpose of this book is to provide an enlightening break in everyday life, and it is not intended to offend or disrespect any individuals or groups involved in historical events.

To Lowan. Thank you, for I have not written or spoken my last words. To Ingvild, for all the love. To Alma and Mille. Look at all the love I´ve found. I love you all. Live now. Flow.

Chapters

Introduction	VII
Joking Before Dying	1
People Named George	20
The Last Supper	26
Jesus Influencers	34
Even More Authors And Poets	46
Answers Before Death	68
When You Know You Are Dying	79
Behave Before Being Beheaded	98
Profanity	104
No Category	109
Life After Death	140
Rest In Power	149
Dying During Christmas	161
On A Final Note	172
Vain Until The End	186
One Last Question	189
Even A Few Sporty People	202

Introduction

In our journey through life, there is one experience we all share: death. It's a universal truth that we will all pass away someday, but it's also something that we often avoid talking about. It's a taboo subject, shrouded in mystery and fear.

But what if I told you that the final words of famous people could shed light on this mysterious subject? What if we could learn from the dying words of those who have come before us and find comfort, humor, and even inspiration in them? That's exactly what this book is about. In the pages ahead, we'll explore the last words of some of the most famous and influential people in history.

From kings and queens to musicians and actors, we'll hear their final thoughts, insights, and even jokes as they faced their mortality. Some of these last words are profound and philosophical, while others are simple and humorous. But each one offers a glimpse into the minds of these iconic figures in their final moments, revealing their fears, regrets, and hopes for the future.

For example, the final words of Marie Antoinette, the last queen of France before the French Revolution, reveal a different kind of perspective. As she climbed the scaffold to be executed by guillotine, she accidentally stepped on the foot of her executioner. Her final words? "Pardon me, sir. I meant not to do it." Despite facing her own death, she remained polite and gracious until the end.

Of course, not all last words are lighthearted. Some reveal the pain and fear that can come with facing death. Others, a mystery. Steve Jobs, the co-founder of Apple and a pioneer in the tech industry, reportedly looked at his family in his final moments and said, "Oh wow. Oh wow. Oh wow."

His last words offer a glimpse into the mystery of death, the unknown that awaits us all. But no matter what kind of last words famous people leave behind, they all offer us a chance to reflect on our own mortality.

By exploring these final utterances, we can confront our own fears and anxieties about death, and find comfort in the shared human experience of facing the end. So, as you read through the pages ahead, I encourage you to reflect on your own mortality. What would your final words be? What kind of legacy would you want to leave behind?

By contemplating these questions alongside the last words of some of history's most famous figures, we can find meaning and purpose in our own lives, even in the face of death.

Ultimately, this book is a celebration of life, even as we confront the inevitability of death. It's a testament to the power of words, and to the enduring legacy of those who have come before us.

So let's dive in, and discover the final thoughts of the famous and the infamous, the wise and the witty, the powerful and the vulnerable.

Let's explore the spectrum of human emotion and experience in the moments before our final breath, and find connection and empathy with those who have faced this same journey.

In many ways, the last words of famous people are a window into the past. They offer a glimpse into the minds of those who shaped our history, revealing their personalities, beliefs, and values. They remind us of the impact that these individuals had on the world, and of the ways in which their legacies continue to shape our lives today.

More than that, the last words of famous people are a reminder of our shared humanity. No matter how famous or successful or powerful we may become, we will all one day face the same inevitable fate. And in those final moments, we will all be vulnerable, scared, and uncertain.

By exploring the final words, we can find comfort in the knowledge that we are not alone in our mortality. We can connect with those who have faced death before us, and learn from their wisdom, humor, and grace.

So, whether you're a history buff, a philosophy enthusiast, or simply someone who wants to better understand the human experience, this book is for you. In its pages, you'll find a wealth of insight and inspiration, as well as moments of laughter and levity.

Above all, you'll discover a shared humanity that transcends time, place, and status. You'll see that, no matter how different we may seem on the surface, we all share a common bond in the face of death. And in that bond, we can find hope, connection, and meaning in the midst of life's greatest mystery.

So come along with me on this journey through the final words of famous people. Let's explore the rich tapestry of human experience, and find comfort and inspiration in the words of those who have come before us. Let's celebrate the beauty and complexity of life, even as we confront the inevitability of death.

Joking While Dying

"I have lived as a philosopher. I die as a Christian.

Giacomo Casanova, an Italian author, died on June 4, 1798. His name lived on as a Casanova. Hardly anyone remembers him as a philosopher or a Christian. According to some, his last words marked the first time he uttered a sentence without trying to get laid. In the 21st century, his name has gradually been replaced with the term Fuckboy.

"Now is not the time for making new enemies.

Voltaire, a French writer famous for his criticism of Christianity, and for his wit, lived up to his reputation on his deathbed. As he lay dying on May 30, 1778, this was his reply when asked to renounce Satan.

The prettier. Now fight for it.

The English dramatist **Henry Arthur Jones** had time to set up one last drama as he spoke his last words on January 7, 1929. His nurse and his niece asked which of them he would prefer to stay with him.

This wallpaper and I are fighting a duel to the death. Either it goes or I do.

Oscar Wilde was staying at the Hôtel d'Alsace in Paris before he died on November 30, 1900. In poor health, he was confined to his room and said to have become fixated on the wallpaper, which he described as hideous. Wilde was never considered a wallpaper, being the wittiest writer of his era and known for his impeccable taste. In his own words, "I have the simplest tastes. I am always satisfied with the best."

Go on, get out! Last words are for fools who haven't said enough!

Marx, the thinker with a grand design, His theories, so revolutionary and divine. He critiqued the system, he railed against the bourgeoisie, A communist utopia, his vision's decree. But alas, his life was filled with strife, And his ideas sparked many a political knife. Yet still today, his words inspire and provoke, As Marx, the theorist, went up in smoke on March 14, 1883.

Ah! A German and a genius! A prodigy—admit him!

Jonathan Swift was an Irish writer best known for his satirical works, including "Gulliver's Travels". His final words on October 19, 1745, were referring to George Frideric Handel, who had come to visit him. Some may think putting German and genius in the same sentence is a satirical highlight.

Remember, Honey, don't forget what I told you. Put in my coffin a deck of cards, a mashie niblick, and a pretty blonde.

He was an American actor and comedian, **Chico Marx**. He said his last joke on October 11, 1961, when he gave his wife instructions for his funeral. It has baffled people ever since. Why did he want to play cards and golf with a seven-iron club with a pretty blonde?

I am curious to see what happens in the next world to one who dies unshriven.

Pietro Perugino, an Italian artist, declining the last rites in 1523.

And if I should ever die, God forbid, I hope you will say: 'Kurt is up in heaven now'.
That's my favorite joke.

Kurt Vonnegut, a literary wit so bright, With words that pierced the darkness of the night. His satirical tales, absurd and sly, Made readers laugh and ponder with a sigh. But life's absurdity, he found in fate, As Vonnegut met his final, humorous state. He was funny as hell until the end on April 11, 2007.

Do you wish to hasten my last hour?

Nicolas Boileau-Despréaux, a poet grand, Whose words could both inspire and reprimand. With satire sharp, he mocked the vices of his time, In rhymes sublime, with wit so prime. But alas, Death's sting, it did befall, As Boileau's muse silenced in the final call. He left the world on March 13, 1711 with a question to a fellow playwright who asked him to read his new play. Not clear if his friend ever wrote a play again.

Someone else can arrange this.

Constance Spry, a floral queen. Her bouquets fit for a royal scene. With artistry and style so grand. She blossomed in the flower land. But life's petals wither, time takes its toll, As Constance's story, sadly, did unfold. Spry died after slipping on stairs while arranging flowers on January 3, 1960.

Nothing more than a change of mind, my dear.

James Madison, the fourth President of the United States, reportedly said this before passing away. It's almost like he was trying to make one final joke before departing this mortal coil. Madison died on June 28, 1836. His health had deteriorated for some time, and his final words were a reply to his niece when asked, "What is the matter, Uncle James?

And now a word from our sponsor.

Charles Gussman, wordsmith on the screen. Crafted tales that made us beam. His scripts brought laughter, tears, and thrills, But life's final scene brought chills. When Gussman was dying, he removed his oxygen mask and said these words on October 18, 2000.

Surprise me.

Bob Hope, from movies to TV, he shone so bright, With humor that soared to dizzying height. Final words spoken on July 27, 2003 after being asked by his wife, Dolores Hope, where he wanted to be buried.

I'd like to thank the Academy for my lifetime achievement award that I will eventually get.

Donald O'Connor. With fame and fortune, Hollywood's delight. His talents shone, a dazzling light. But life's stage can be fickle and grim, His final bow, a sad requiem. Last words spoken to his family at his bedside on September 27, 2003.

My last words will be 'Hoka Hey, it's a good day to die.' Thank you very much. I love you all. Goodbye.

Clarence Ray Allen, a cunning crook. His rap sheet long, his name in every book. From schemes to fraud, he played a wicked game. But soon, justice caught up with his infamous name. A life of crime, with consequences dire. His final words, a lament for his expired fire. A cautionary tale, a felon's fall from grace, A lesson learned, in life's ruthless race. Final statement written prior to execution by lethal injection on January 17, 2006.

Tape Seinfeld for me.

Harvey Korman, a comedic king, Brought laughs to all with every zing. From "Carol Burnett Show" to "Blazing Saddles", His humor left us in hysterics, no battles. A master of wit, with impeccable timing, His legacy lives on, a comedic gem worth rhyming. Did not watch Seinfeld after May 29, 2008.

Well, I've got to be alive for it, haven't I?

Prince Philip, the royal charmer. Sported a sharp wit with a farmer's armor. As Duke of Edinburgh and Prince Consort, he faced scandals and quips of every sort. His dry humor and gaffes made many chuckle. A true royal jester, with a wit that would buckle. The prince was talking to his son, then Prince of Wales, now King Charles, about Phillip's 100th birthday, which would have taken place 2 months and 1 day after his death on April 9, 2021.

Can you turn rainy weather into dry?

Heraclitus, the pondering sage. Philosopher of the ancient age. His thoughts were deep, his words profound, But rarely with a smile, he was found. With fire as his cosmic theme, his wisdom shone with an inner gleam. He left us pondering life's grandest riddle, with a smirk on his face and a cryptic middle. With his last words he was asking his physicians for relief from dropsy in 475 BCE.

It is better to perish here than to kill all these poor beans.

Pythagoras, the mystic math man, his teachings spread across the land. With triangles and numbers divine, he sought the truth in every line. But alas! His followers grew unruly, his theories deemed too lofty, too truly. Yet his legacy lives on today, in math class horrors that won't fade away. He was refusing to escape with his students from the Crotonians through a fava bean field before dying in 495 BCE.

How can the teeth of wild beasts hurt me, without consciousness?

Diogenes, the cynic, so bold and absurd, living in a barrel, like a free-thinking nerd. He mocked social norms with his biting wit, lived like a beggar, not giving a shit. But when he died, his friends were in distress, for finding a barrel-sized coffin was a serious mess! Diogenes was asking for his body to be thrown outside the city wall for animals to eat before dying in 323 BCE.

Alexander the Great, so grand and bold, conquered lands and stories were told. From Macedonia to Persia, he did march, leaving foes in his fiery arch. But, in Babylon, his journey did cease, leaving his empire without a lasting peace. His legacy lives on, yet his fate is clear, even the great can't escape death's looming fear. Spoke his last words when asked to whom his vast empire should belong after his death on June 11, 323 BCE.

Lorentzos Mavilis, a poet so bright, his words flowed freely, a literary delight. With rhymes and verses, he painted his tale, but life's trials and tribulations, they did assail. Though his poems lived on, his time was brief, as death came knocking, a somber motif. Yet his legacy shines, in literature's embrace, A satirical ode, to his poetic grace. He experienced his final greek tragedy on November 29, 1912.

Félix Arvers, a French poet and dramatist, revealed his secret while dying on November 7, 1850. Charles X restricted the freedom of the press, dissolved the newly elected Chamber of Deputies, and changed the electoral laws to favor the wealthy. Charles X's actions were a threat to the constitutional monarchy and the principles of democracy, and his reign was marked by controversy and scandal.

Demonax, the Cynic sage, roamed the streets with wit and rage. Mocking conventions, he was a thorn, in society's side, all day till morn. His sardonic humor, a cutting knife, made the high and mighty question life. But when death came, with its final blow, He left behind a legacy that continues to grow when he died around year 170 CE.

I am roasted,—now turn me, and eat me.

Saint Lawrence, deacon, with zeal aflame, stood up to Rome's oppressive claim. Asked for riches, he brought a grill, proclaimed, "I'm done, please have your fill!" Mocked and roasted, he kept his grin, even in death, he won with a sinfully good spin. Last words spoken on August 10, 258 CE while being burned alive.

It is not painful, Paetus.

Arria, Roman woman (42 CE), to her husband, Aulus Caecina Paetus. Aulus had been condemned to death but given permission to kill himself. When he hesitated to do so, his wife stabbed herself first and handed the dagger to him.

I wished to do more harm than I could.

Ranulf Flambard, clever and sly, with power and wealth, he reached the sky. Bishop of Durham, a master of schemes, amassing riches beyond his wildest dreams. In government, he played the game, but his deeds led to a fiery, scandalous claim. Behind bars, he learned a lesson grim, crime doesn't pay, even for a bishop so slim. Last words before dying on September 5, 1128.

Will not all my riches save me? What, is there no bribing death?

Henry Beaufort, a churchman's role. With political power, he did extol. Bishop of Winchester, rich and grand, a puppet master, pulling strings with his hand. From council chambers to royal courts, his influence rose to great reports. But in the end, life's fleeting breath, A reminder that power ends in death on April 11, 1447.

I have offended God and mankind because my work did not reach the quality it should have.

Leonardo da Vinci, a Renaissance man, with talents unmatched, a genius plan. From paintings to inventions, a polymath bold, his genius revered, a story oft told. But in the end, mortality did prevail. A life well-lived, a creative tale. As he painted and pondered, he left his mark, a timeless legacy, in art and arc. Last words spoken on May 2, 1519 to King Francis I of France.

I desire to go to hell, and not to heaven. In the former place I shall enjoy the company of popes, kings, and princes, while in the latter are only beggars, monks, hermits, and apostles.

Niccolò Machiavelli, a political wiz, His treatises on power, a cunning biz. His "The Prince" proclaimed ruthless ways, To gain and maintain power all his days. But when his time came, he met his end, His dark wit lives on, a Machiavellian trend. Spoke his last words on June 21, 1527.

I would say 'somewhat,' but I cannot utter it.

Henry Frederick, Prince of Wales, heir apparent, Brilliant, talented, with a royal warrant. His legacy lost, a future once bright, Taken by illness, a cruel blight. Oh, what could have been, we'll never know, A prince departed, a kingdom's woe. Last words spoken on November 6, 1612 when asked if he was in pain.

Already my foot is in the stirrup.

Miguel de Cervantes, Spain's literary sage, a master of the quill, an author all the rage. Don Quixote, his famed and chivalrous tale, inspiring readers, a literary sail. His legacy lives on, his words still told, A writer immortal, a legend of old. Final words on April 22, 1616.

All right then, I'll say it. Dante makes me sick.

Lope de Vega, the playwright supreme, with words that danced and plots that gleam. A prolific pen, a talent so bright, he ruled the stage with sheer delight. His legacy lives on, a thespian's dream, A maestro of wit, a theatrical theme. Last words before he passed away on August 27, 1635.

Nothing succeeds with me. Even here, I meet with disappointment.

Mikhail Bestuzhev-Ryumin, a Russian officer, when the rope broke during his hanging for having helped organize the Decembrist revolt, on July 25 1826.

Stay for the sign.

Charles I, the royal king. With subjects, he could not bring. Agreement, strife, and woe, Resulted in his overthrow. His legacy, a tragic tale, of power struggles that did fail. Beheaded, lost his throne, a cautionary tale well known. Last words asking for his executioner to await his signal before beheading him on January 30, 1649.

I know you are here to kill me. Shoot, coward, you are only going to kill a man.

They were only killing one man on October 9, 1967, **Che Guevara**. What they did not know was that they would drown the entire world with t-shirts bearing his face, worn by millions of teens not having the slightest clue what it symbolized. Well, how could they know. It is mostly known as a fashion statement.

I did not mean to be killed today.

Henri Turenne, the noble lord, Warrior skilled with sword and word. He led his troops with great acclaim, His legacy, a storied name. But in the heat of battle's might, He met his end in tragic fight. His valor sung, his deeds revered, A legend lost, a hero's fate feared. Final words spoken moments before he was struck by a cannonball at the Battle of Salzbach on July 27, 1675.

Well, ladies, if I were one hour in heaven, I would not be again with you, as much as I love you.

Mary Rich, the Countess bold, Her beauty shone, worth untold. Her parties grand, her wit renowned, A socialite, the toast of town. Her wealth and charm, a potent force, Yet death did come, as no remorse. Her legacy, a lavish life, Now remembered with awe and strife. Last words spoken before dying on April 12, 1678.

I knew it! I knew it! Born in a hotel room and, goddamn it, dying in a hotel room.

Hate it that happens! **Eugene O'Neill**, American playwright, to his wife Carlotta Monterey, November 27 1953.

There are six guineas for you, and do not hack me as you did my Lord Russell. I have heard that you struck him three or four times. My servant will give you more gold if you do your work well.

James Scott, 1st Duke of Monmouth, illegitimate son of Charles II of England.Last words spoken on July 15, 1685, to Jack Ketch, his executioner. Ketch was nervous and took several blows to behead Scott.

I have been a most unconscionable time dying, but I beg you to excuse it.

Charles the Second. His legacy, a playboy's tale, of parties wild, and wines so stale. Restored to throne with merry cheer, But died and left us, all in fear. A king so charming, yet so flawed, His legacy, a royal facade. Last words before dying on February 6, 1685.

More weight.

Giles Corey, a farmer, meek and mild, accused of witchcraft, went on trial. Pressed with heavy stones, he stood his ground, with wit and humor, he astounded. His legacy, a tale of might, a farmer's fight against the blight. Though crushed to death, he'll never tire, in folklore, he'll live, a witch trial satire. Final words spoken before being pressed to death during the Salem witch trials on September 19, 1692.

Promise me you will never again marry an old man.

William Wycherley, a witty bard. Wrote plays that pushed the boundaries hard. His bawdy comedies, a scandalous hit, poking fun at the upper class twit. Though his work was bold, he fell from grace, his legacy lives on, a satirical embrace. Spoke his final words on January 1, 1716 to his wife. He had married a much younger woman less than twelve days before his death.

Ain't they darlin'?

Sally Basset, a slave with no voice. Her struggles and pain, we can't rejoice. Her legacy of strength and defiance, a symbol of resistance, a beacon of alliance. Her death, a tragic chapter in history's scroll. Her story lives on, a testament to the soul. Spoke her final words on June 6, 1730, while looking at the logs prepared to fuel her burning at the stake for poisoning.

Oh Lord! Forgive the errata!

Andrew Bradford, a man of print, a publisher with wits and hint. His legacy, the press he ran. With news and ads, a bustling plan. His death, a loss to the print industry, but his papers live on, with journalistic synergy. Last words before he died on November 24, 1742.

I see that you have made three spelling mistakes.

Thomas de Mahy, a Marquis of old, his legacy, tales of treacherous gold. He met his death, a gruesome fate, condemned to hang, a tragic state. His name lives on, in history's page, a cautionary tale, for the next stage. Spoke his last words upon reading his death warrant on February 19, 1790.

I did, sir, but you do now.

William Ledyard, a soldier brave and true, fought for freedom, red, white, and blue. In Connecticut's militia, he did rise, but alas, met his demise. His legacy, valor and might. Fighting for his country's right. A hero's story, though he fell, his memory, in history's spell. He was surrendering Fort Griswold during the Battle of Groton Heights. The British officer to whom Ledyard gave his sword in surrender immediately killed him with it.

If you wait a little, I shall be able to tell you from personal experience.

Gluck, a composer known to fame. Italian and French operas his claim to name. With music that stirred the soul and heart, his legacy, a melodic work of art. His death, though mourned by many a fan, his music lives on, in eternal span. Spoke his last words on November 15, 1787, when asked whether a tenor or a bass should sing the role of Christ in The Last Judgement.

Waiting, are they? Waiting, are they? Well, God damn 'em, let 'em wait!

Ethan Allen, a patriot bold and true, led the militia with a fervent cue. Fighting for freedom, he took a stand, a legacy left across the land. But alas, death's call, it could not wait, Ethan Allen, an American hero's fate. Final words on February 12, 1789, on being told the angels were waiting for him.

Let my epitaph be, 'Here lies Joseph, who was unsuccessful in all his undertakings.'

Joseph the Second, the Emperor great. Wielded power with an iron state. Reforms aplenty, he did try. But often met with a dubious sigh. His legacy mixed, with praise and critique. Joseph the Second, an Emperor unique! But alas, the end, it came too soon, His reign cut short, by death's cold swoon on February 20, 1790.

I'll be shot if I don't believe I'm dying.

Edward Thurlow, a lawyer with a fearsome rep. Barrister extraordinaire, adept. But in politics, his skills did shine. As Britain's Lord Chancellor, he did dine. His legacy, a mixed bag indeed. Some praised, some scorned, for his deeds. Yet in the end, he met his fate. Leaving behind a political debate on September 12, 1806.

I believe we shall adjourn this meeting to another place.

Adam Smith, the economist so wise. With "The Wealth of Nations" to his prize. His "invisible hand" and free-market lore. Made him a thinker that many adore. But when he met his final fat, his legacy continued to debate after he spoke his last words on July 17, 1790.

A dying man can do nothing easy.

Ben Franklin, the polymath with wit so keen. Inventor, statesman, a man widely seen. His kite-flying antics and lightning rod fame. Brought electricity to his impressive name. But alas, old age finally took its toll, And Franklin passed on, a genius of soul. His final words on April 17, 1790 complaining about the difficulty of assuming a more comfortable position on his deathbed.

No, whatever is, is best.

Theophilus Lindsey, a man of faith, so true. Unitarian beliefs he did pursue. His legacy, a liberal voice. Challenging orthodoxy, a daring choice. Though scorned by some, he stood his ground. In life and death, a rebel profound. Last words spoken on November 3, 1808 to a friend who suggested that Lindsey was strengthened by the saying, "Whatever is, is right".

I am not coward, but I am so strong. It is hard to die.

Meriwether Lewis, the explorer, so bold and brave. His legacy, vast lands he did pave. From the Mississippi to the Pacific shore. He blazed trails, and tales galore! But mystery shrouds his death so grim. A tragic end for one who charted the whim. Final words spoken on October 11, 1809, before dying of suicide or possible murder.

That is surprising, since I have been practicing all night.

John Philpot Curran, with wit so bright. A politician, orator of might. In Irish courts, he held his sway. His eloquence a dazzling display. His legacy, a silver tongue's delight. A champion of rights, a beacon of light. But time took its toll, as years went by, Curran's voice stilled, his wit did die. His final joke was said on October 14, 1817, when his doctor said he was coughing "with more difficulty".

Wolcot's pen, sharp as a sword. In satirical jests he struck with word. Mocking society, he spared no one. From king to courtier, he had his fun. His legacy, satirical lore. A wit that cut, left hearts sore. Death took him, but his words still sting, Wolcot's satirical legacy, an everlasting thing. Final words spoken on January 14, 1819 when asked, "Is there anything I can do for you?".

If any of you have a message for the devil, give it to me, for I am about to meet him!

Lavinia Fisher, a tale so grim. Accused of murder, cold and grim. A serial killer, or just a myth? Her legacy, a chilling mythos, a mythic myth. Her life cut short, by the hangman's noose. Or was she innocent? Who's to deduce? Last words spoken prior to execution by hanging on February 18, 1820.

Perhaps some day they will hear my music without even saying 'Poor Bellini'.

Poor **Vincenzo Bellini**, composer of fame. His legacy, melodies that earned him acclaim. With operas beloved, a master of the art. But his life cut short, it broke every heart. An early death, a tragic loss, Yet his music lives on, a timeless boss. Spoken before dying on September 23, 1835.

Ah, very well.

Thomas Arnold, famed for his school's reign. Legacy of learning, they did attain. A master of history, a pedagogic guide. Yet his own death, a sorrowful tide. His teachings live on, but alas, he's gone. A scholar's life, a legacy that lives on ever since Arnold spoke his final words on June 12, 1842 to his physician, who had described his serious prognosis and treatment.

Surrender? Your grandmother should surrender, you bastard!

Eduardo Abaroa, Bolivian hero of the War of the Pacific (23 March 1879), responding to Chilean forces asking him to surrender. Known as the creator of the Your Grandma-jokes, the predecesor to the Your Mama-jokes.

Are you sure it's safe?

A doctor by day, a killer by night, **William Palmer's** deeds, a dark and twisted sight. With potions and poisons, he played his part. Taking lives with his sinister art. But justice prevailed, his guilt was found. His legacy, a notorious renown. Spoke his last words on June 14, 1856, to the hangman while looking at the trapdoor on the gallows.

Ah, Luisa, you always arrive just as I'm leaving.

Massimo d'Azeglio, from politics to art, he was the man. A Renaissance soul with a master plan. He painted, he wrote, he led the way. But alas, death came to end his day. His legacy lives on, a polymath's delight. An Italian luminary, shining bright. His final words was spoken on January 15, 1866, when seeing his estranged wife arrive at his bedside as he died.

I do not have to forgive my enemies. I have had them all shot.

Ramón María Narváez, the Duke of Valencia so grand. A Spanish general, mighty in command. Prime Minister he was, with power untold. But alas, his legacy tarnished, his deeds bold. His death, a reminder, power's fleeting guise, A lesson for those who chase the prize. Words spoken before he died on April 23, 1868.

No, it is better not. She will only ask me to take a message to Albert.

Benjamin Disraeli, the Prime Minister bold and wise. A master of wit and political guise. His life, a tale of charm and ambition. A legacy of shrewdness and tactful volition. But alas, his death, a final cessation, Leaving behind a nation in deep contemplation. Disraeli Declined a visit from Queen Victoria with his last words on April 19, 1881.

That was the right prayer.

Jay Cooke, the financier of fame, Built his fortune on Wall Street's game. But market crashes and financial woes. Brought an end to his legacy's glows. His wealth, once vast, now but a vapor. A tale of a greedy caper. Having overheard a prayer for the dead, this was his last response on February 16, 1905.

Here lies one whose name was written in hot water.

Robbie Ross, Canadian-British journalist, art critic and art dealer before dying on October 5, 1918. He was referring to the inscription on John Keats' grave ("Here lies One Whose Name was writ in Water»).

Kill me, or else you are a murderer!

Franz Kafka's life, an existential twist. His legacy, a literary abyss. A Kafkaesque world of absurdity. In his works, a reflection of reality. His death, a mystery left unsolved, Like his stories, a puzzle yet unresolved. Asking his doctors for morphine overdose while dying of tuberculosis on June 3, 1924.

I am starting to believe you are not intending to count me among your friends!

Pedro Muñoz Seca, the playwright so witty. With comic works that were oftentimes gritty. Satirical jabs, sharp and incisive. His legacy, plays so hilariously divisive. But alas, his life met a tragic end. Assassinated by foes, a playwright's mournful trend. His comedic legacy lives on with laughter. A playwright remembered for wit ever after. Final words was to his firing squad during the Paracuellos massacres, on November 28, 1936.

I'll need it.

Folke Bernadotte, a diplomat so grand. With peace in mind, he'd take a stand. Nobleman by birth, humanitarian by heart. Seeking to heal conflicts, a noble art. Legacy of peace, his work well-known. His death by assassins, a tragic tone. Yet his efforts for harmony, a lasting trace. In a world oft marred by strife and chase. His last words on being wished good luck by a journalist prior to his assassination on September 17, 1948.

__All the damn fool things you do in life you pay for.__

Édith Piaf, a voice so strong and pure. Her songs could make hearts ache and cure. Her life, a tale of highs and lows. From the streets of Paris to worldwide shows. Legacy of music, her gift divine. Her death mourned, but her voice still shines. Final words spoken to her sister before dying on October 10, 1963.

__This is my final word. It is time for me to become an apprentice once more. I have not settled in which direction.__

Max Aitken, the media tycoon supreme. With newspapers and power, a formidable theme. His life full of deals and political clout. Aitkens legacy, a media empire, no doubt. But alas, even the baron met his final fate, For all his wealth and power couldn't cheat death's date on June 9, 1964.

__Absolutely not!__

Montgomery Clift, an American actor, to his private nurse, Lorenzo James July 23, 1966. She had suggested they watch The Misfits on television.

__Capital punishment; them without the capital get the punishment.__

John Spenkelink, a man of strife. Convicted of a heinous crime, a darkened life. His days behind bars, his fate was sealed. For murder committed, a fate revealed. Yet controversy loomed, protests ran high. A story that left many asking why. His death, a somber end to a tragic tale. A reminder of crime's dark and twisted veil. Spoken prior to execution by electrocution on May 25, 1979.

__I'm bad, I'm nineteen.__

Phil Lynott, rock 'n' roll's charming bard. A voice that struck a chord, a rockstar's card. Thin Lizzy's frontman, a legend's name. A poet's soul, set hearts aflame. His legacy lives on in songs so sweet. A rocker's heart, forever will beat. Lynott died at age 36 on January 4, 1986.

Yeah, country music.

Buddy Rich. Final words to a nurse who asked him, "Is there anything you can't take?" He then died during surgery on April 2, 1987.

I'd hate to die twice—it's so boring

Richard Feynman, a brilliant mind. Theoretical physicist of a one-of-a-kind. With wit and charm, he'd spin a tale. His legacy, a scientific trail. From quantum realms to bongo drums. His genius left us in awe, it hums. Though he's passed, his spirit bright. Forever shines in scientific light. Said his last joke on February 15, 1988.

I'll finally get to see Marilyn.

Joe DiMaggio, a baseball ace. He swung the bat with skill and grace. But fame's game also played its part. With Marilyn Monroe, a doomed sweetheart. Together, they made the headlines gleam. A love story that was quite extreme. Now they're gone, but their tale still rings. In tabloids and baseball lore, it clings. Last words before dying on March 8, 1999.

O, holy simplicity!

Jan Hus, a theologian bold and wise. Challenged the church with a critical guise. His fiery sermons, his writings bold, made some folks gasp, and others scold. But Hus refused to back down, you see, till he was burned at the stake, tragically. His legacy of reform, a spark, still shines today, though in the dark. While being burned at the stake for his belief, Hus saw an old woman throw a small amount of brushwood onto the fire, and his final remarks on July 6, 1415, can still light up someones day!

Only one man ever understood me. And he really didn't understand me.

Georg Wilhelm Friedrich Hegel, a philosopher quite profound. In dialectics, he was renowned. With his complex thoughts, he'd oft confuse, But his legacy, it still accrues. His death, no simple end in sight, His dialectical journey, day and night, ended November 14, 1831.

I would never have married had I known that my time would be so brief. If I had known that, I would not have taken upon myself double tears.

Alexis, a Tsar of olden days, married his wife in a lavish craze. But wedded life was not so grand, as tensions rose across the land. Their rule was met with discontent, and legacies that came and went. In the end, their story told. Of power, love, and dynastic mold. But history, with its mocking smirk, reminds us all: beware the perks. Spoken before his death on February 8, 1676.

Not...

Robert Emmet, a rebel true. Fought for Ireland, through and through. His oratory skills were grand. But his uprising was soon banned. His legacy, a martyr's tale, of defiance, courage, and fail. His death, a tragic end, they say, yet his spirit lingers to this day. Last words spoken during execution by hanging for treason. The executioner carried out the hanging in the middle of Emmet's attempt to say "Not yet" for the third time on September 20, 1803.

What an irreparable loss!

Auguste Comte, the French philosopher of his day, sought to order the world in a new way. Positivism was his grand scheme, but his social theories caused a gleam In the eyes of some, while others frowned, yet his legacy in thought is still renowned. As for his death, he passed with grace, leaving a legacy that finds its place since September 5, 1857.

Shoot straight, you bastards. Don't make a mess of it!

Breaker Morant, the man of controversy, a military officer with a dark history. Accused of war crimes, he stood in court, his legacy debated, with opinions sought. Did he deserve praise, or should he be shamed? A life of war and death, his fate proclaimed. In the end, he faced a bitter end. A legacy clouded, around which debates still wend. Last words to to his firing squad on February 27, 1902.

People Named George

Show my head to the people. It is worth seeing.

Georges Danton, a leading figure in the French Revolution, was vain until his last breath on April 5, 1794. There are no existing photographs of Georges Danton, as he lived before the invention of photography and even before Tinder, so there is no proof he had many matches. However, contemporary descriptions of Danton suggest that he was robust and charismatic, known for his powerful oratory and imposing presence. Danton was said to have had a large frame and a round, friendly face, with a prominent nose and deep-set eyes. While there is no universal agreement on whether he was conventionally handsome, many historians and contemporaries have noted his compelling and forceful presence, which likely contributed to his popularity and influence during the French Revolution.

I die hard, but I am not afraid to go. I am just going. Have me decently buried, and do not let my body be put into the vault in less than two days after I am dead. Do you understand me? 'Tis well.

George Washington, the father of America and a true American hero. Because nothing says "accomplishment" like owning a bunch of slaves and being really good at chopping down cherry trees. His last words were reportedly spoken to his attending physician, Dr. James Craik, on the evening of December 14, 1799, shortly before his death.

Well folks, you'll soon see a baked apple.

George Appel, an American murderer, prior to execution by electrocution on August 9, 1928.

Lo! here is a token that I forgive thee; my heart, do thine office.

George Wishart, a preacher true. Called for change, the Gospel's due. With fiery sermons, he denounced the Pope. Challenging Catholicism, giving them hope. But persecution followed fast, accused of heresy, it wouldn't last. Imprisoned, condemned, his fate was sealed, martyred for his beliefs, a Protestant zeal. Wishart was kissing one of his executioners on the cheek after the man asked for his forgiveness.

I'm tired. I'm going back to bed.

George Reeves, the Superman star, with a cape and tights, he'd go far. He leapt tall buildings, faster than a train, until one day, things took a dark strain. Mysterious death, a Hollywood mystery, rumors abound, a cloud of history. Reeves' legacy, a fallen hero's tale, a legend lost, a somber, tragic veil. Final words prior to his suspected suicide on June 16, 1959.

To my friends / My work is done / Why wait? / G.E.

George Eastman, American entrepreneur (14 March 1932) and founder of Kodak. Eastman invited some friends to witness a change of his will. After some conversation and light-hearted joking, Eastman asked them to leave. Moments later, he shot himself once in the heart with an automatic pistol. His final words was left in a suicide note.

O God! I am dying. (To his physician:) This is death.

George IV, a king in name, known for his flamboyant fame. Legacy of lavish living, debts, mistresses, all unforgiving. A king of excess, a royal show, but his reign, marred by scandal's blow. George IV, a king's demise, Leaving behind a tarnished prize. Spoken moments before he died on June 26, 1830.

It matters little to me; for if I am but once dead they may bury me or not bury me
as they please. They may leave my corpse to rot where I die if they wish.

George Buchanan, a scholar profound. With intellect vast, his knowledge renowned. A historian, humanist, a man of letters, intriguing minds with his scholarly fetters. From Scotland's history to Europe's lore, he left his mark, that's for sure. But death's cold grip, it came one day, bidding farewell to a scholar's display. His last words spoken on September 13, 1582, when his servant asked who would pay for his burial after Buchanan told him to distribute his property among the poor.

Don't die like I did.

George Best, a Northern Irish football player before he died on November 25, 2005. He died as an indirect result of alcoholism. An estimated three million people still die as he did. His final words have gone largely unnoticed compared to his alcohol-praising funny one-liners. Quotes like "I spent a lot of money on booze, birds and fast cars. The rest I just squandered" and "In 1969 I gave up women and alcohol - it was the worst 20 minutes of my life" are being used as sad excuses by alcoholics to undermine their drinking problem to this day.

Love one another.

George Harrison, the "Quiet Beatle," played guitar, From Liverpool's fame to Eastern star. Taxman came, cancer too, But George's spirit always true. He spoke his last words to his wife, Olivia Harrison, and son, Dhani Harrison on November 29, 2001.

Dear world, I am leaving because I am bored. I feel I have lived long enough. I am
leaving you with your worries in this sweet cesspool — good luck.

George Sanders, British actor. Debonair and sly, onscreen villain, oh, so spry. Charmed the ladies with his wit, a silver-tongued and dashing Brit. But fame's facade, a lonely place. Life's emptiness he couldn't chase. Tired of it all, he took his leave, An enigmatic end, some still believe. Last words written in a suicide note. Sanders died on April 25, 1972.

Stop, go out of the room; I am about to die.

George Fordyce, a healer renowned. With stethoscope and wisdom profound. A Scottish physician, skilled and bright, diagnosed with wit, cured with might. He spoke his final words on May 25, 1802 to his daughter, who had been reading to him.

Tell them I have a great pain in my left side.

George Eliot, Eliot, the pen name of Mary Ann. A literary genius, a brilliant plan. From Middlemarch to Silas Marner. Her novels captivated, a literary charmer. But scandalous affairs, a satirical tale. As Eliot's life had a twist, a scandalous trail. Her unconventional choices, frowned upon. Yet, her writings endure, a legacy won. Final words on December 22, 1880.

I love you, too.

George H.W. Bush, the 41st President of the United States, reportedly said "I love you too" to his son before passing away. It's almost like he was trying to get in one last "I love you" before his final exit as if that would absolve him of all the policies and decisions he made during his presidency. His legacy remains a mixed bag, but at least he went out on a sentimental note on November 30, 2018.

My dear, before you kiss me good-bye, fix your hair. It's a mess.

George Kelly, wordsmith bold and grand. With scripts that made us laugh and understand. On stage he shined, a talent rare. With wit and humor beyond compare. But alas, his final curtain call drew near. A legacy of laughs, forever held dear. Last words spoken to one of his nieces before dying on June 18, 1974.

Farewell, I am going to die. Goodbye Lina, goodbye Maurice, goodbye Lolo, good ...

George Sand, a writer of fiery words. Her tales captivating like singing birds. With pen as her sword, she fought for change, Her legacy, stories that still estrange. But life's complexities, hard to deny. Love, loss, scandal, as time went by, her passions burned, her flame grew bright, Till death's curtain fell, a final night on June 8, 1876.

Is this death?

George Lippard, an American author and labor organizer, asked his physician this on February 9, 1854. It was, indeed, death.

Nurse, it was I who discovered leeches have red blood.

Georges Cuvier, the zoologist king. With fossils and creatures, a scholarly fling. His studies were groundbreaking, his knowledge vast. But his theories at times, a bit too fast. From classifying species to extinction's claim. His contributions brought him fame. Yet, his own demise, a final jest, as death outwitted, the man who knew best. Cuvier spoke his last words on May 13, 1832 to a nurse who was bleeding him.

Sister, you're trying to keep me alive as an old curiosity, but I'm done, I'm finished, I'm going to die.

George Bernard Shaw, the witty bard, penned plays that cut through the avant-garde. His words sharp as knives, his satire biting, challenging societal norms with humor, quite inviting. But alas, his curtain closed, his final bow, a legend in theater, both then and now. Shaw's legacy lives on, his words still provoke, a playwright extraordinaire, a literary stroke! Last words spoken on November 2, 1950, to his nurse.

I am in a cold sweat. Is it the sweat of death? How are you going to tell my father?

Georges Bizet, the French composer of Carmen, died tragically at the age of 36. He reportedly worked himself to death, trying to finish his last opera, The Pearl Fishers. Rumor has it that he was so frazzled that he even started conducting with a baguette instead of a baton. Spoke his last words before dying on June 3, 1875.

This is a hell of a way to die.

George S. Patton loved the battle cry, A general whose courage soared high. From North Africa to Normandy's shore, His troops followed him, forevermore. But victory's glory was not enough, Patton's temper could be rough. Injured in a car crash, he met his fate, Leaving behind a legend that couldn't wait on December 21, 1945.

At fifty, everyone has the face he deserves.

George Orwell, a wordsmith bold. His pen was sharp, his stories told. Of dystopian worlds, oppressive states. Where truth was mangled by those in fates. His wit and satire cut so deep, awakening minds from slumber's sleep. Though gone from earth, his words live on, a beacon of truth that still shines on. Final words before he passed away on January 21, 1950, at the age of 46.

Ay! but I have been nearer to you, my friends, many a time, and you have missed me.

George Lisle, a Royalist leader in the English Civil War. His legacy shines in battles fought, for the crown, he valiantly wrought. But alas, defeat was his fate, in Civil War's tumultuous state. Now history remembers his name. As a fallen leader in the game. Final words on August 28, 1648), when the officer in charge of his firing squad said they would hit him.

It is a great mystery, but I shall know all soon.

George Peabody, a banker grand. Known for wealth, he'd lend a hand. Generous gifts, philanthropic acts, endowed great causes with impactful pacts. But when he died, his riches told, the court contested, the heirs were bold. A legal tussle, a bitter fight, For George Peabody's vast estate's right! Last words before dying on November 4, 1869.

The Last Supper

Hey, fellas! How about this for a headline for tomorrow's paper? 'French Fries!

James French, an American murderer on August 10, 1966, when asked if he had any last words before his death by electric chair.

The nourishment is palatable.

Millard Fillmore, the 13th President of the United States, is proof that anyone can achieve greatness with a solid combover and a love of compromise. He managed to keep the country from tearing itself apart during the turbulent pre-Civil War era, but his legacy is largely overshadowed by his unremarkable name. He suffered a stroke in February 1874 and died on March 8. He was commenting on the soup he had eaten before he passed away.

Water.

Ulysses S. Grant, the renowned general and 18th president of the United States, was a man of many talents. He could lead an army, run a country, and hold his liquor better than most - but not in his dying moments. He died of throat cancer on July 23, 1885, and spoke his last word when asked if he wanted anything.

Give me a large cup of tea.

John George Wood. Author, and very British, until his end on March 3, 1889.

Pity, pity - too late!

Ludwig van Beethoven, a German composer, was informed that his publisher had gifted him 12 bottles of wine on March 26, 1827.

It's a long time since I drank champagne.

It is always too long ago since we all had champagne. Hopefully, **Anton Chekhov**, a Russian author, had time for some bubbles before dying on July 15, 1904.

It was the food!

Richard Harris was a famous Irish actor who passed away on October 25, 2002. According to some reports, his last words as he was being wheeled out of the Savoy Hotel in London were "It was the food!». Some have suggested that he was making a lighthearted comment about the quality of the food at the hotel, while others have interpreted the remark as an indication that his poor diet may have contributed to his declining health. Harris was known for his wit and sense of humor, so it's possible that his final words were simply meant as a quip or a joke. (Please do not sue me, Savoy).

Bring me a glass of Champagne.

William Price. From herbal cures to flamboyant attire, A maverick doc, a rebellious fire. A proponent of cremation, he fought the norm, Burning his dead son, a controversial form. Despite legal battles and societal frown, a funeral pyre, for Price, would be his renown. Price prioritized life one last time on January 23, 1893.

Damn. This is funny.

Doc Holliday, a gambler's ace. With cards and guns, he'd set the pace. From the Wild West's saloons to showdowns dire, a quick-draw maverick, with nerves of fire. He spoke his last words after a nurse refused him a whiskey on November 8, 1887.

An olive, with a pit...

Victor Feguer, an American convicted murderer requested his last meal before execution by hanging on March 15, 1963.

Ah, that tastes nice. Thank you.

Johannes Brahms, a maestro's touch. With notes and chords, he'd create so much. A grumpy genius, with wit and style. His melodies live on, bringing smiles. Final words spoken after being given a glass of wine before dying on April 3, 1897.

It would be hard indeed if we two dear friends should part after so many years, without one sweet kiss.

Turlough O'Carolan, a bard so bright. With melodies that took flight at night. From harp strings plucked with skill and grace. A composer's legend, in Ireland's embrace. Last words spoken to a bowl of wine he was no longer able to drink on March 25, 1738.

Crito, we owe a cock to Asclepius. Please, don't forget to pay the debt.

Greek philosopher Socrates, who was known for his unconventional ideas and questioning of traditional beliefs, had made quite a few enemies in Athens. Eventually, these foes managed to bring him up on charges of corrupting the youth and impiety, accusing him of spreading dangerous ideas and undermining the authority of the state. Socrates, never one to back down from a challenge, defended himself vigorously in court, even though he was offered the chance to flee into exile. Sadly, despite his eloquent and compelling arguments, the jury found him guilty and sentenced him to death in 399 BCE. The last words were spoken just before the ingestion of poison hemlock which he was forced to drink as a death sentence.

Let's have a really good red wine tonight.

Carl Jung, the psychoanalyst supreme. A dream interpreter, a mind to gleam. From archetypes to collective unconscious, a brilliant mind, sometimes contentious. With Freud's disciple, then a split. A pioneer's journey, a mind's great fit. Exploring psyche's depths, he'd delve. A psychoanalyst's tale, a mind's upheaval. Last words before taking his last sip on June 6, 1961.

This to the fair Critias.

Theramenes, an Athenian sage. In politics, he'd dance and engage. From democrats to oligarchs, he'd sway. A master manipulator, come what may. But in the end, his fortunes wane, as power games, they shift and change. Accused of treason, his fate was sealed. A statesman's tale, the truth revealed. Spoke his last words after swallowing poison hemlock which he had been condemned to drink by Critias in 404 BCE.

One last drink, please.

Jack Daniel, was an American alcohol businessman and founder of the worst whiskey in the world. Last words spoken before dying on October 10, 1911. With its distinct taste and iconic square bottle, JD has become a staple of American drinking culture. Sure, it might not be the fanciest or most refined whiskey out there, but hey, at least it's reliable. Cheers to you, Jack, for leaving us with a legacy of questionable decisions and regrettable hangovers.

I did not get my Spaghetti-Os. I got spaghetti. I want the press to know this.

Thomas J. Grasso, American double murderer, prior to execution by lethal injection on March 20, 1995. No one cared, Thomas.

While you're about it, sir, you might make that a double.

Neville Heath, English double murderer. Heaths last words was spoken when he was offered a drink prior to his execution by hanging in Pentonville Prison on October 16, 1946.

Go and give the ass a drink of wine to wash down the figs.

Chrysippus, a Greek philosopher, had a party before dying of laughter in 206 BCE.

Prepare cognac, see you tomorrow!

Vladislav Volkov, Soviet cosmonaut on June 30, 1971, during his final transmission from Soyuz 11 prior to fatal reentry.

My boy, the quenelles de sole were splendid, but the peas were poor. You should shake the pan gently, all the time, like this.

Marie-Antoine Carême, a culinary maestro. A French chef, a gastronomic manifesto. From Napoleon's feasts to grandiose soirées, his creations amazed, in delectable arrays until he died on January 12, 1833. His last words were spoken to a pupil.

I think I could eat one of Bellamy's veal pies.

William Pitt, the Younger, a British wunderkind. Prime Minister at just twenty-three, oh, how time flew blind. He faced war, debt, and political strife, a prodigy's burden, throughout his life. But alas, his health began to fray. As stress and toil took their toll, day by day. Though his star shone bright, it dimmed too soon, a political prodigy, a star-crossed boon. Last hungry on January 23, 1806.

Wish I had time for just one more bowl of chili.

Kit Carson, a legendary frontiersman of lore. A rugged explorer, always wanting more. From trapping to guiding, he made his way. Through wild landscapes, come what may. Final words spoken before dying on May 23, 1868.

My exit is the result of too many entrées.

Richard Milnes, a poet and politico. With verses and speeches, a formidable duo. From rhymes to rhetoric, he had a way. With words and wit, come what may. But politics can be a treacherous game, even for a poet with a noble name. Baron Houghton's life, a blend of art and state, a funny tale, both witty and great. Spoke his last words before dying on August 11, 1885.

Codeine... bourbon.

Or like Hunter S. Thompson would call it: Breakfast. **Tallulah Bankhead**, an American actress before dying on December 12, 1968.

Whatever you would like me to have.

Maurice Baring, a man of letters so bright. With wit and wisdom, a literary light. From novels to poems, he wrote with grace, a wordsmith extraordinaire, a true literary ace. Gave his last answer on December 14, 1945, when asked what he wanted for lunch.

I should have had the pickle.

Preston Sturges, a playwright with a comedic flair, his works were witty, beyond compare. With clever dialogues and humorous scenes, he brought laughter to screens and theater screens. Spoke his last words before dying on August 6, 1959.

Drink to me.

Pablo Picasso, famed art maestro. With a brush that danced, a mind that'd go. Cubism, Surrealism, his trade. Revolving styles that never fade. But life's palette changed, and time did slay. The master's last masterpiece, the grave's display April 8, 1973.

It must have been the coffee.

Jack Soo, a TV star. With humor sharp, he'd go so far. Detective Yemana, witty lines, jokes and puns that aged like fine wines. But fate's cruel hand, it did unfold, the curtain closed, the story told on January c11, 1979. Soo was referring to the bad coffee Soo's character made on the sitcom Barney Miller.

I want the world to be filled with white fluffy duckies.

Derek Jarman, film's avant-garde. A maverick mind, bold and bizarre. Queer themes, art-house flair, provocative, with style so rare. But life's reel ended, the director's chair, had these final words on February 19, 1994.

Quick, quick! some vinegar! I am fainting.

Joseph Fourier, math's luminary. Transformed heat with math, extraordinary. Fourier series, waves and heat. Calculus feats, truly elite. But his time came, a final cessation. Leaving us puzzled with his math equation. Last words spoken was on May 16, 1830, calling to his physician, who had stepped out of the room.

Oh Puss, chloroform—ether—or I am a dead man.

Richard Francis Burton, a man of might. A polymath with passions to ignite. From exploring lands to mastering tongues, his thirst for knowledge never stung. But, his journey met its end, A polymath's tale, an illustrious blend, on October 20, 1890. Last words to his wife, Isabel Burton.

Bing Crosby, crooning star of old. With smooth voice, he struck pure gold. From "White Christmas" to "Swinging on a Star," his songs traveled near and far. But one fateful day, his voice did fade, leaving us all serenely dismayed. Crosby spoke his final words on October 14, 1977, moments before collapsing and dying of a heart attack.

Jesus Influencers

It is finished.

Possibly one the the first ever known Jesus influencers, it is reported that these words were the last **Jesus** spoke right before his death by crucifixion in 30 CE. It was, however, not finished. It was the birth of Jesus influencers - where one's faith is measured by the number of likes, shares, and followers they have on social media. These social media superstars can turn even the most mundane Bible verse into a viral meme, complete with perfectly filtered images and clickbait headlines. You've got the "prayer warriors" who will pray for you if you follow them back, the "holier-than-thou" types who claim to have all the answers to life's big questions, and the "Godly gains" enthusiasts who somehow manage to incorporate a Bible verse into every workout post. But let's not forget the influencers who have taken "prosperity gospel" to a whole new level - promising their followers that if they donate enough money to their "ministries," God will bless them with wealth and success. Because apparently, Jesus' message of humility and service to others really meant "show off your fancy car and designer clothes on Instagram. And of course, no Christian influencer's account would be complete without the occasional "I'm not perfect, but I'm forgiven" post, conveniently posted right after a scandal or controversy. Because in the world of Christian influencers, it's not about actually living a life of faith and authenticity - it's all about maintaining the illusion of perfection and righteousness. But hey, who needs a personal relationship with God when you can just buy your way into heaven with Instagram followers and sponsored posts.

Oh, Lord God Almighty, as thou wilt!

James Buchanan, the 15th President of the United States, left behind a legacy as impressive as his ability to do absolutely nothing. Despite being in office during one of the most tumultuous periods in American history, he managed to sit back and let the country fall apart. He died from respiratory failure caused by pneumonia on June 1, 1868, in Lancaster, Pennsylvania.

I'm gonna go see Jesus, want to see Jesus.

Whitney Houston, diva supreme. Her voice soared high, a pop music dream. Grammy wins, stardom bright. But fame's dark side, a harrowing plight. From hits to scandals, paparazzi chase, her personal struggles, a public disgrace. Drugs and drama, a rocky road, a voice silenced, a tragic ode. Houston supposedly said this to friends the day before she died on February 11, 2012.

Goodbye, all, goodbye. It is God's way. His will be done.

William McKinley, the 25th president of the United States, is remembered for his achievements in the art of handshaking and the invention of the high-five. He also managed to win the Spanish-American War, but let's be honest, that was mostly due to the fact that Spain's navy was made of paper mache. On September 6, 1901, McKinley was shot twice by Leon Czolgosz. He died from his injuries on September 14.

Then to our blessed Lady Mary, the mother of God, I commend myself. May she, by her holy intercessions, reconcile me to our Lord and Savior, Jesus Christ. God be merciful to—

William the Conqueror, a Norman Duke. With ambition and strategy, he struck like a fluke. He won England's crown, with power and might, but ruling was tough, a daily fight. Feuds and revolts, a royal mess. Marital woes, a source of stress. Conquests and clashes, wars to be won, William's reign, a tale of battles and fun. But time took its toll, as it always does, even kings succumb to nature's laws. Death came calling, the conqueror fell, leaving a legacy, a medieval tale to tell. Last words spoken after hearing the bell ringing Prime on September 9, 1087.

What the devil do you mean to sing to me, priest? You are out of tune.

Jean-Philippe Rameau, a composer bright. With harpsichord keys, he'd tickle just right. His music, complex, harmonies grand. But critics scoffed, "too avant-garde for the land!» A musical genius, ahead of his time. But royalties scarce, his pockets would mime. He passed away, his fame obscure. Now revered as a master, music's allure. He spoke his final words on September 12, 1764 to his confessor.

God does not die!

Gabriel García Moreno, former President of Ecuador, left behind a legacy as impressive as his extensive collection of religious relics. He ruled the country with an iron fist, but also managed to bring stability and progress to a nation in turmoil. His legacy includes being remembered as a saint by some and a tyrant by others, but mostly as that guy who really liked religious statues. Moreno was assassinated in Quito on August 6, 1875.

Jesus, I love you.

Nothing quit says Jesus influencers like being The Pope! Pope **Benedict XVI**, a pontiff so wise, guiding the Church with a watchful guise. Conservative stances, doctrinal might, but scandals rocked, an unholy sight. Resignation, a papal first, a life of piety, now immersed. Retired in prayer, a quiet abode. Spoken before dying on December 31, 2022.

You know not what you do.

Nicholas II, a Tsar in his prime. An autocrat ruling in a lavish clime. But discontent brewed, unrest seethed. Revolution struck, the monarchy seceded. Imprisoned, abdicated, a royal fall, a tragic end to the Romanovs' hall. Executed with his family, a somber fate. The last Emperor's dynasty, sealed by hate. The last Emperor of Russia, and his family were executed by Bolshevik revolutionaries on July 17, 1918. Nicholas was quoting Jesus upon being informed he and his family were to be put to death.

Lord Jesus, receive my spirit. Lord, lay not this sin to their charge.

Saint Stephen, a deacon of the early Church. With faith and fervor, he'd always lurch. But preaching truth, it ruffled feathers, religious leaders, their patience tethers. Accused of blasphemy, a grave offense, A kangaroo court, no recompense. Stoned to death, a martyr's end. His legacy lives, a spiritual trend. Saint Stephen, an early Christian deacon, when stoned to death in 34 CE.

God help me, for I am innocent.

Zulfikar Ali Bhutto, the former prime minister of Pakistan, is remembered for his flamboyant style and his political machinations. He also managed to put Pakistan on the map with his nuclear program, which is like getting a gold star for building a bomb that could destroy the world. His legacy is complicated, but at least he gave us something to talk about besides cricket. He spoke his last words before his execution by hanging on April 4, 1979.

Jesus.

King Edward III, a royal charmer, His reign was long, a regal armor. From the Hundred Years' War to the Black Death, His kingdom faced challenges with every breath. Conquests and campaigns, a knightly quest, But wars and plagues, they put him to the test. Edward's rule, a mixed bag of glory and strife, A monarch's rollercoaster, the ups and downs of life. Spoken before he kissed a crucifix and died on June 21, 1377.

Ah, Jesus!

King Charles V, a ruler bold and grand, conquered lands with an iron hand. But wars and politics took their toll, he tired of the throne, losing control. Retired to a monastery, oh so serene, No more kingship, just a humble scene. In solitude, he found his peace. A king who abdicated, seeking release. Words spoken before his last breath on September 16, 1380.

Though He slay me, yet will I trust in Him.

It's like the ultimate game of trust fall, except you're falling into the loving arms of an all-powerful deity who might smite you for the fun of it. But who needs a safety net when you've got blind faith, as **Grace Aguilar**, an English author, dying on September 16, 1847

Lord, into Thy hands I commend my spirit.

Charlemagne, the great Frankish king. An empire vast, a glorious thing. Conquests and coronations, a mighty feat. But managing lands, a royal heat. With warring vassals and restless states, he ruled with force, tried to placate. But all good things must come to an end, Charlemagne's death, a final trend. He quoted Jesus before dying on January 28, 814.

I've always loved my wife, my children, and my grandchildren, and I've always loved my country. I want to go. God, take me.

Dwight D. Eisenhower, the 34th president of the United States, is remembered for his military leadership during World War II and his love of golf. He also warned us about the military-industrial complex, which is like warning someone about a tiger in their backyard and then giving them a steak to throw at it. His last words, reported to be, "I want to go. God, take me," which is a sentiment shared by anyone who ever had to deal with Congress. Dwight D. Eisenhower, the 34th president of the United States, had been suffering from heart failure before he died on March 28, 1969.

I HAVE HAD A HAPPY LIFE AND THANK THE LORD. GOODBYE AND MAY GOD BLESS ALL!

Chris McCandless, American hiker who wrote this final note before dying on August 18, 1992. He died of starvation, or poisoning from seeds or plants. McCandless story later became well known with the film Into The Wild. He died despite of being in an area full of hunters, near a river full of fish and was only living 10 miles from a highway. So, naturally he became a wilderness hero. Ever since McCandless fans and pilgrims attempting to retrace his journey have been lost, injured, and at least two been killed.

I know only Jesus the crucified.

Wessel Gansfort, a theologian bright. A humanist with ideas in flight. But his views, they challenged the norm. Orthodoxy frowned, a brewing storm. Critics clashed, debates abound, Wessel stood his ground, unswayed and sound. His legacy, a mind ahead of his time, a Dutch humanist, with ideas sublime. Spoken before running out of ideas on October 4, 1489.

My Lord died innocent of all crimes, for my sins; and shall not I willingly give my soul for the love of Him.

Girolamo Savonarola, a friar with fire. Preached reform, a zealous desire. Condemning sins, from Florence's pulpit. Challenging excess, he wouldn't quit. But his strict rule, it rubbed some wrong. Critics rose, a dissenting throng. Accused of heresy, a fatal blow, Savonarola's fate, a tragic show. Burned at the stake, his voice was stilled, a Dominican friar, whose fire was filled. A radical figure, ahead of his time, Savonarola's legacy, a complex paradigm. Said his final words on May 23, 1498, when asked before his execution if he was resigned to death.

I come. I come. It is right. Wait a moment.

Pope Alexander VI, a pontiff with flair. Indulged in excess, beyond compare. Borgia by name, Borgia by nature. Papal scandals, a twisted feature. Nepotism, bribery, and cunning plots, unholy deeds in papal lots. His reign, a tarnish on the Church, Alexander VI, a pope in lurch. Death claimed him, a fitting end. A pope whose legacy, hard to defend. Last words spoken before dying on August 18, 1503.

Into Your hands, O Lord, I commend my spirit.

Columbus, the explorer bold and keen. Sailed the seas, seeking lands unseen. "New World" he claimed, a grandiose boast. But Native peoples, a tragic cost. Conquistadors followed, plundered with might. Colonization, a dubious sight. His legacy debated, a complex view, Columbus, the explorer, with a controversial hue. Columbus quoted Jesus before dying on May 20, 1506.

Leo X, a pope of lavish ways. Indulged in luxuries, throughout his days. Patron of arts, a connoisseur, but funds he lacked, a papal blur. Indulgences sold, a papal scheme, to fill the coffers, a papal dream. Reformation sparked, a blow to his might, Leo X's papacy, a tumultuous sight. Death claimed him, a pope with flair, Leo X's legacy, a complex affair. A pope of excess, a man of vice, a strong tale, of papal dice. Leo was rumored to have died by poison on December 1, 1521.

Patrick Hamilton, a cleric pure. Preached reform, with passion sure. But Church authorities, with ire, Branded him a heretic, to conspire. His teachings radical, a threat perceived. Inquisition's flames, he believed. Martyrdom claimed him, a tragic fate, Hamilton's legacy, a Church debate. Spoke his final words while being burned at the stake 29 February 29, 1528.

Zwingli, a priest, with zeal ablaze. Reform ideas, he did raise. A voice for change, a Protestant fire. Challenged Rome, with strong desire. But Swiss Cantons, divided and torn, Zwingli's dreams, were partly shorn. In battle fought, a fatal blow, Zwingli fell, a Reformer's woe. Mortally wounded at the Battle of Kappel, he spoke his last words on October 11, 1531.

John Hooper, a bishop, stern and stout. Spoke out against Rome, without a doubt. Sentenced to die, he faced the stake, in sarcastic tones, he made them quake: "Make sure the fire is hot and bright, For I'll be roasting Protestant tonight!". With his last words he was refusing a pardon prior to burning at the stake for heresy on February 9, 1555.

That is enough to last till I get to Heaven.

Warham, the Archbishop, prim and proper. A pious figure, like no other. Crowned Canterbury's spiritual guide, Till death's dark shadow, by his side. His legacy, a church's might. Intrigue and politics, a holy fight. But Warham's reign, a mortal tale. A funny spin, on Canterbury's trail. Last words spoken on August 22, 1532 when a servant told him he had thirty pounds left.

Lord, open the King of England's eyes.

Tyndale, a scholar, a Bible's bard. Translated scripture, with utmost regard. But the Church, with power and might, labelled him a heretic, a rebellious sight. His works banned, his life in strife, Tyndale paid the ultimate price, with life. Yet his words, they spread like wildfire, a striking ode, to a translator's ire. Last words before being strangled and burned at the stake for heresy on October 6, 1536.

Did you envy my happiness?

Francisco de San Roman, a merchant bold. A Protestant heart, of faith untold. He traded goods, with shrewd finesse. But the Inquisition, brought him distress. Accused of heresy, his fate was dire, he met his end, in martyr's pyre. A satirical lament, for a merchant's plight, in Spain's religious turmoil, a somber light. While burning at the stake in the year 1540, he moved his head in a way which caused the friars to believe he had recanted. Upon his removal from the flames, he asked them this question and was then returned to the fire.

We are beggars, this is true.

Martin Luther, a reformer, with fire in his voice. Nailed theses, made the Church his choice. He sparked a revolution, a Protestant fire. But life was tough, as tensions grew higher. Excommunicated, condemned to die. His last words spoken, a satirical sigh on February 18, 1546.

Let the flames come near me. I cannot burn! I cannot burn!

Nicholas Ridley, Bishop bold and wise. Championed reform, to his own demise. Condemned to burn, he faced the pyre, with wit and humor, did he inspire: "I pray thee, light the fire with speed, For this old body is in great need!" While burning at the stake for heresy on October 16, 1555, only his lower limbs burned away.

Like Peter, I have erred, unlike Peter, I have not wept.

Stephen Gardiner, bishop in power. A master of politics, a scheming tower. He played his cards, with shrewd deceit, a Catholic stalwart, ruthless and discreet. But in the end, his fortunes waned, his legacy tainted, his influence drained. A figure of intrigue, in the annals of lore, a bishop who played, but won no more. Spoke his last words on November 12, 1555.

It is time for Matins.

John of the Cross, a mystic divine. Contemplative priest, in quiet shrine. With pen and prayer, he sought the light. Through dark nights, he faced the fright. His words inspired, his faith profound. Till death embraced, this saintly sound. Now his legacy lives, in hearts and minds. A beacon of faith, that forever shines. Spoke his last words when dying at the stroke of midnight. (Matins is a Christian service of morning prayer).

I die a martyr and willingly — my soul shall mount up to heaven in this chariot of smoke.

Giordano Bruno, a friar so bold. With a mind that questioned and ideas untold. He sought to explore the cosmic skies, with his thoughts that challenged church's lies. But his views were seen as heresy, and he faced the church's tyranny. Burned at the stake, his fate was grim, yet his spirit of inquiry still shines within. Words spoken on February 17, 1600, prior to burning at the stake for heresy.

Thy creatures, O Lord, have been my books, but Thy Holy Scriptures much more. I have sought Thee in the fields and gardens, but I have found Thee, O God, in Thy Sanctuary—Thy Temple.

Francis Bacon, known for his wit. A philosopher of great intellect. He wrote essays, he dabbled in law. But his quest for knowledge had a flaw. His experiments, so grand and bold. Led to an untimely death, we're told. For testing meat's preservation, he caught a chill, a grave situation. Alas, his life, cut short too soon, by the pursuit of scientific boon on April 9, 1626.

I have kept the faith once given to the saints; for the which cause I have also suffered these things; but I am not ashamed, for I know whom I have believed, and I am persuaded that He is able to keep that which I have committed to Him against that day.

William Bedell, bishop wise and sage. Served Kilmore in a bygone age. With pen and parchment, he translated, the Bible, for which he's celebrated. But alas, his efforts met a cruel fate, for opposing the King's religious state. Arrested, imprisoned, his health did wane. In Kilmore, he died, a martyr's stain. Final words spoken on February 7, 1642 before dying from exposure after being imprisoned and tortured by rebels.

My work is done; I have nothing to do but to go to my Father.

Selina Hastings, of noble birth. Had a religious zeal that shook the earth. Countess turned preacher, methodist divine, her sermons drew crowds in every shrine. A champion for faith, a beacon of light, her legacy shines, even in the night. Last words spoken before dying on June 17, 1791.

Why, certainly, certainly!

Taylor, a preacher, with fervor preached. His Methodist faith he firmly reached. His sermons roused many souls to pray. But alas, he met an untimely fray. A life cut short, a tragic end, leaving his flock to mourn and rend. Final words spoken when a friend asked him if Jesus was precious on April 6, 1871.

Here I am finally. Here I am at the end of the tumultuous career that, whatever my repugnance, I have kept to for so long. My troubles will soon be over and my true happiness is coming, since I have all confidence in the mercy of my God. I willingly leave this world where I have been thought happy in that I have had public admiration, been respected by great, esteemed kings. I can't say that I regret all these honors—it's just that they add up to vanity and trouble.

Pigneau de Behaine, a missionary bold. Left France to spread the faith, we're told. In Vietnam he toiled, with passion ablaze, converting souls in far-off Asian days. His life was a quest, a zeal so bright, but sadly, he passed into eternal light. Last before dying in Vietnam on October 9, 1799.

There is no such thing as sudden death to a Christian.

Wilberforce, the Anglican bishop divine. His sermons flowed with eloquent shine. With passion and zeal, he spread the word, but life's journey was not always stirred. A fall from a horse, a fateful blow, His earthly days came to a woe. A bishop's life, a final chapter, Leaving his flock in sorrowful rapture on July 19, 1873.

Guard the Church I loved so well and sacredly.

Pius IX, a pope with a lengthy reign. Like an ironclad, he held his domain. With dogma and doctrine, he stood strong, but progress and change, he did prolong. Till his last breath, he held the throne. Infallible, but not quite prone. A pope for the ages, or so they say. Till death claimed him and took his sway on February 7, 1878.

Let me go to the house of the Father.

Pope John Paul II, a papal force. His papacy, a global discourse. From Poland's land, he rose to might, championing faith, both day and night. But time caught up, age took its toll, and death embraced this holy soul. With sadness, the world bid adieu, to a pope who left a papal view. Spoke his last words on April 2, 2005.

I have loved justice and hated iniquity; therefore I die in exile.

Gregory VII, a pope so bold and stern, A reformer with a fiery concern. He clashed with kings and wielded might, For church supremacy, he'd fight. But in the end, his power did wane, Leaving behind a legacy of pain. A pope who dared to challenge the might, But met his match in life's last fight on May 25, 1085.

Even More Authors and Poets

Well, I must arrange my pillows for another night – when will this end!

Washington Irving, an American writer, before his last pillow fight on November 28, 1859.

Take away those pillows. I shall need them no more.

Lewis Carrol, an English author who could not be bothered before dying on January 14, 1898.

Let me have my own fidgets.

Walter Bagehot, British journalist, businessman and essayist (24 March 1877), declining help rearranging his pillows. Possibly foreseeing how impossible it would be to get hold of a Fidget spinner in 2018.

Did the doctors really say I was not to get up?—If they said so, then I won't get up; but I feel well.—No, I will keep them [the pillows] as the doctors left them.

Sir Andrew Agnew, 7th Baronet, Scottish politician on April 28, 1849.

Don't worry, be happy.

Chances are you will not know your last words until it is too late. **Meher Baba** might hold the world record for time knowing. The Indian spiritual master last spoke on July 10, 1925. After this, he observed silence for the rest of his life until he died 44 years later, on January 31, 1969.

Goodnight my kitten.

American author **Ernest Hemingway** possibly challenged the world to write a story in three words before taking his own life with a shotgun on July 2, 1961.

The priest could never draw another thing from dying but 'Dear Sir, you are so kind.'

Louis Petit de Bachaumont, a man of noble birth, was known for his "studied indolence" and his role in the gossipy Mémoires secrets. He was also an arbiter of taste, an influential art critic, and an urbaniste. His life was full of intrigue and scandal, but his death was unremarkable. Perhaps he was too busy gossiping to notice his own demise. He spoke his final words on April 29, 1771.

I want, oh, you know what I mean, the stuff of life.

Bayard Taylor, a writer of travel lore, Voyaged the world, his tales galore. With wit and wisdom, he shared his quest, His legacy, a travelogue's zest since December 19, 1878.

O, that beautiful boy!

Ralph Waldo Emerson. A transcendentalist, a thinker profound. His essays and poems, a wisdom profound. His death at seventy-eight, a loss so great, but his legacy, eternal, continues to fascinate. Spoke his last words on April 27, 1882.

Charge, young man!

José Martí, a Cuban hero of great fame. Fought for freedom, his writings aflame. Though his life cut short, his spirit lives on, his legacy, a symbol of resistance, a shining dawn. Final words on May 19, 1895, addressing trooper Angel de la Guardia during the Battle of Dos Ríos.

What can happen to me? I can only die.

Edward Bellamy, a visionary of the past. Wrote of a utopia that forever will last. His "Looking Backward," a captivating tale, a future world where social progress would prevail. Final words before dying on May 22, 1898.

Thy will be done.

Lew Wallace, a man of many pursuits. A soldier, lawyer, and writer with creative fruits. "Ben-Hur," his epic tale of chariots and Rome, a literary triumph, a sensation to enthrone. Final words spoken on February 15, 1905.

It is no use fighting death any more.

John Millington Synge, a writer with a lyrical voice. Captured the Irish soul in every poetic choice. "Playboy of the Western World," his comedic feat, a story of a hero's rise and fall that can't be beat. Died on March 24, 1909.

God will help me. I am so tired.

Julia Ward Howe, a poet and suffragist bold. Her words and actions, a story to be told. "Battle Hymn of the Republic," her famous verse, A patriotic anthem that could pierce and rehearse. Last words before dying on October 17, 1910.

Take courage, Charlotte; take courage.

Anne Brontë, a talented writer, overlooked in her time. Her works deemed too tame, a feminist paradigm. Her early death at twenty-nine, a tragic loss. Now her legacy revered, a feminist cause. Final words spoken on May 28, 1849, to her sister Charlotte.

Oh, I am not going to die, am I? He will not separate us. We have been so happy.

Charlotte Brontë, the famed author of Jane Eyre. Wrote tales of Gothic passion that set hearts afire. Her life, a melodrama with love and heartbreak, her works, a literary treasure, her legacy, no mistake. Her death at thirty-eight, a bitter pill to swallow, her brilliance, unmatched, but fame's wheel is hard to follow. Last words on March 31, 1855, addressing her husband Arthur.

While there is life there is will.

Patrick Brontë, a reverend with three gifted daughters. Their literary fame, a tribute to his parenting orders. His life, a humble tale of faith and strife, but the Brontë legacy, a literary life. The father of Charlotte, Branwell, Emily and Anne Brontë spoke his last words on June 7, 1861.

Everything is atoned for.

August Strindberg, a playwright with a tormented mind. His dramas and prose, a reflection of a troubled find. From "Miss Julie" to "A Dream Play" so surreal, his works, a glimpse into the human psyche's ordeal. Died on May 14, 1912.

Arthur, don't look at me! Nurse stand between my brother and me.... Jesus, Mary and Joseph, I give you my heart and my soul.

Robert Hugh Benson, a priest and author renowned. His novels and writings, a literary treasure to be found. From "Lord of the World" to "The Necromancers" so grand, his stories, a thrilling journey, a spiritual wonderland. Died on October 19, 1914.

So here it is at last, the distinguished thing.

Henry James, an American-British sage. Wrote tales of intrigue on each and every page. From "The Turn of the Screw" to "The Portrait of a Lady," his works, a literary treasure, oh so shady. Last words before dying on February 28, 1916.

I am only asking for one thing—let me finish my work.

Isaac Babel, a writer with a bold voice. His stories, a reflection of his time and choice. From "Red Cavalry" to "Odessa Stories" so fine, his works, a literary treasure that will forever shine. Last words spoken on January 27, 1940, prior to execution by firing squad on fabricated charges of terrorism and espionage.

What a life!

Radclyffe Hall, a literary trailblazer. Her novels, bold and without a waiver. "The Well of Loneliness," a groundbreaking tale, her life, a story of resilience that will never fail. Died aged 63 on October 7, 1943.

I can't hear very well. And there's a mist in front of my eyes. But it will go away, won't it? Don't forget to open the window tomorrow.

Boris Pasternak, a poet with a soul so bright. His words, a literary beacon, a dazzling light. From "Doctor Zhivago" to lyrical verse, his works, a captivating, poetic universe. Died on May 30, 1960.

Human life is limited; but I would like to live forever.

Yukio Mishima, a writer and provocateur. His works, a literary venture, rich and pure. With samurai ideals and a controversial flair, his life, a tale of passion and despair. His death at forty-five, a shocking end, a final act, a message to send. Last written words prior to seppuku on November 25, 1970. Seppuku is the honourable method of taking one's own life practiced by men of the samurai (military) class in feudal Japan.

A certain butterfly is already on the wing.

Vladimir Nabokov. From "Lolita" to "Pale Fire" in his hand, his works, a captivating wonderland. His life, a journey of artistic grace, with twists and turns, a thrilling chase. Final words spoken on July 2, 1977. He had a keen interest in butterflies.

I did what I could.

Edward Abbey, nature's wild voice. His life, an adventure, a daring choice. From canyons to mountains, he roamed free, entertaining, rebellious, a legend to be. Died on March 14, 1989.

Capitalism... Downfall.

Christopher Hitchens, a wordsmith's delight. Debating and writing with all his might. From politics to religion, he'd never shy, a provocative mind that made us sigh. Final words spoken to his agent Steven Wasserman on December 15, 2011.

Well, my friend, what news from the Great Mogul?

François de La Mothe Le Vayer, a thinker quite rare. With skepticism and wit, he'd snare. Challenging norms, beliefs, and creeds, In satirical style, he'd plant his seeds. From philosophical debates to worldly affairs, his pen and tongue, sharpened with flares. Last words on May 9, 1672, to physician and traveler François Bernier, who had come to say goodbye to him.

God bless you, my dear.

Samuel Johnson, the greatest man of letters in English history, was known for his wit, his love of tea, and his impressive dictionary. He rose from obscurity to become a literary giant, but his life was not without its struggles. Despite his fame, he died in relative obscurity, leaving behind a legacy that would inspire generations of writers to come. Dying on December 13, 1784, he spoke his last words to Miss Morris, a young woman.

I can't anymore.

James Beard, culinary king, foodie's delight, an entertaining fling. From cookbooks to TV, his fame did expand, a gastronomic journey that will forever stand. Last words on January 23, 1985, before he was no longer able to speak.

I am grateful to Divine Mercy for having left me sufficient recollection to feel how consoling these prayers are to the dying.

Jean-François de La Harpe, a French critic and unsuccessful playwright, was known for his severe and provocative criticisms of French literature. He was orphaned at a young age and imprisoned for allegedly writing a satire against his protectors at college. Despite his bitterness, he wrote many uninspired plays, with his first tragedy being perhaps his best. He was respected but often disliked for his unsympathetic views and died in Paris in 1803, leaving behind a legacy of caustic criticism. His final recorded words, spoken the day before his death on February 11, 1803.

Taught, half by reason, half by mere decay, / To welcome death, and calmly pass away.

Arthur Murphy, an Irish writer, was known for his short biography of Samuel Johnson and his pseudonym Charles Ranger. He was a gifted student of the Latin and Greek classics, but his career path was less clear. He worked as an actor, a barrister, and a journalist before finally becoming a writer. With his last words on June 18, 1805, he was quoting Alexander Pope.

Remember me as a revolutionary communist.

Leslie Feinberg, an American transgender activist, communist, and author on November 15, 2014.

My beautiful flowers, my lovely flowers!

Jean Paul, German Romantic writer on November 14, 1825, touching a wreath of flowers he had been given. Jean Paul had lost his senses of sight and smell before his death.

It comes at last, the happy day: Let thanks be given to God in heaven, while we learn pleasure in His way.

Agrippa d'Aubigné, a French poet, soldier, propagandist and chronicler dying on April 29, 1630.

Do open the shutter in the bed-room, in order that more light may enter.

Johann Wolfgang von Goethe, the last Renaissance man. Was a German writer, scientist, and statesman, widely regarded as the greatest and most influential writer in the German language. Some of his works was considered dark, but he wanted light as he left earth on March 22, 1832.

Pull up the shades; I don't want to go home in the dark.

William Sydney Porter, better known as O. Henry, lived a life of irony and coincidence. His stories romanticized the commonplace, but his use of surprise endings cost him critical favour. He died in 1910, leaving behind a legacy of dry humour and a gift for storytelling. Last words on June 5, 1910, to a hospital nurse.

Death is the great key that opens the palace of Eternity.

John Milton, an English poet and intellectual before dying on November 8, 1674.

When I think of the existence which shall commence when the stone is laid over my head, how can literary fame appear to me, to any one, but as nothing? I believe, when I am gone, justice will be done to me in this way — that I was a pure writer. It is an inexpressible comfort, at my time of life, to be able to look back and feel that I have not written one line against religion or virtue.

Thomas Campbell, a who was known for his forgetfulness and occasional silence. His ancestors' elopement with a Kilpatrick girl improved the family's living standards. His written testimony was a sweetener of private life. Last words spoken on June 15, 1844.

Lord, help my poor soul.

Edgar Allan Poe, known for his dark and brooding tales. Spent his life oscillating between literary genius and financial ruin. Despite his love for alcohol and opium, he managed to pen timeless classics like "The Raven" and "The Tell-Tale Heart." Unfortunately, his untimely death in 1849 is shrouded in mystery, much like the endings of his own stories. Last words known spoken before dying on October 7, 1849.

Now comes good sailing. Moose...Indian.

Henry David Thoreau, the nature-loving transcendentalist, spent his days in the woods, scribbling in his journal and espousing self-reliance. His masterpiece "Walden" extolled the virtues of simple living, yet he relied on his mom's laundry service. His civil disobedience led to jail time, and his death in 1862 left us pondering, "Did he die of beans or boredom?». Final words on May 6, 1862.

Ah! my child, let us speak of Christ's love—the best, the highest love!

Fredrika Bremer, the famous Swedish writer, championed women's rights and social reform in the 19th century. She left a lasting legacy as a trailblazer for female empowerment, showing the world that women could be literary powerhouses too, much to the dismay of the gender norms police. Last words spoken on December 31, 1865.

All mortal!

Gustavo Adolfo Bécquer, the renowned Spanish poet, lived a life as dramatic as his poetry. He was notorious for his love affairs, his melancholic musings, and his disdain for conformity. His poems were a melancholic symphony of unrequited love, heartbreak, and existential ponderings. Sadly, his untimely death at the age of 34 left the literary world in mourning on December 22, 1870. Last words spoken in a delirium from fever.

To be a gringo in Mexico – ah, that is euthanasia!

Ambrose Bierce, a master of satire in his writing and life alike. Known for his biting commentary on society, he lived a life filled with snarky observations, sharp-tongued critiques, and sardonic wit. His mysterious disappearance in 1913, never to be seen again, left the literary world in suspense, wondering if he simply found the ultimate punchline to life's absurdities or became the subject of his own dark humor. Bierce wrote his last words before his disappearance in Mexico.

Well, they have got us. They are a damn sight worse than I ever thought they were.

Elbert Hubbard, the prolific writer and philosopher, was a man of many talents and opinions. His witty and often controversial writings lampooned societal norms and skewered the status quo. Final words on May 7, 1915, before dying with his wife in the sinking of the RMS Lusitania. "They" was referring to the German Empire.

There does not seem to be anything to do.

Alice Moore Hubbard, an American feminist and writer on May 7, 1915, on her husband being asked "What are you going to do?" prior to the sinking of the RMS Lusitania.

Put that bloody cigarette out!

Saki (Hector Hugh Munro), a British writer. Last words spoken on November 14, 1916, prior to being killed by a German sniper during the Battle of the Ancre in World War I.

Take a step or two closer, lads. It will be easier that way.

Erskine Childers, the Irish author, and politician, led a life that could rival the plot of one of his espionage novels. From his early days as a British naval officer to his later career as an advocate for Irish independence, Childers was known for his biting wit and clever satire. He spoke his last words facing a firing squad on November 24, 1922.

I believe… I'm going to die. I love the rain. I want the feeling of it on my face.

Katherine Mansfield, the famed New Zealand author, was as rebellious in life as she was in her cutting-edge writing. Her bohemian lifestyle and tempestuous relationships were the talk of literary circles, as was her penchant for biting social satire. Her untimely death from tuberculosis at the age of 34 left the literary world mourning on January 9, 1923.

Everything's gone wrong, my girl.

Arnold Bennett, famous for his novels and essays, lived a life of luxury and privilege. He spent his days hobnobbing with the elite, sipping champagne and nibbling on caviar, all while writing about the plight of the common man. When he died, his estate was worth millions, proving that writing about the poor can be quite profitable. His last words on March 27, 1931, was spoken to his mistress, Dorothy Cheston.

If you survive, never forget what is happening here, give evidence, write and rewrite, keep alive each word and each gesture, each cry and each tear!

Simon Dubnow, a Jewish-born Russian historian, writer and activist. Spoke his last words on December 8, 1941, prior to his murder in the Riga ghetto at the time of the Rumbula massacre.

Doctor, do you think it could have been the sausage?

Paul Claudel, the French poet and playwright. He wrote some of the most boring plays and poems that ever existed. If there was an award for most tedious writing, he would have won it several times. Despite his lack of creativity, he managed to gain some popularity in his time. But let's be real, nobody remembers him now except for the few scholars who have to suffer through his work. Last words spoken on February 23, 1955.

The only objection against the Bible is a bad life.

John Wilmot, 2nd Earl of Rochester and an English poet and courtier dying on July 26, 1680.

Mama— Mama— Mama.

Truman Capote, an American author on August 25, 1984. He had been separated from his mother for several years during his childhood.

You made one mistake. You married me.

Brendan Behan, the Irish playwright and poet. He was known for his wild ways, endless drinking, and reckless behavior. His life was a series of drunken misadventures and colorful anecdotes that would put even the most outrageous reality TV show to shame. As for his death, well, it was no surprise that it came early due to his lifestyle choices. But hey, at least he lived his life to the fullest, or at least until the next pub closed. Sláinte, Brendan! He spoke his last words to his wife Beatrice, on March 20, 1964.

I were miserable, if I might not die.

John Donne, an English poet, scholar and soldier on March 31, 1631.

Excuse my dust.

Dorothy Parker - the queen of sass and wit, known for her sharp tongue and biting humor. Her life was a whirlwind of booze, bad decisions, and brilliant writing, which often got her into trouble. She once said, "I don't care what is written about me as long as it isn't true," which pretty much sums up her approach to life. Died on June 7, 1967.

It is stuffy, sticky, and rainy here at present – but forecasts are more favourable.

J.R.R. Tolkien, the author who made us all believe that a bunch of hobbits could save the world. It's a good thing he didn't live to see all the unnecessary sequels and spinoffs of his beloved trilogy. Final words written in a letter to his daughter Priscilla before dying on September 2, 1973.

This is where the real fun starts.

Ben Travers - the master of farce and wit. What can I say about the man who gave us "Rookery Nook" and "A Cuckoo in the Nest"? Well, he was a writer, of course, but more than that, he was a master of the absurd. And let's not forget, he was a fan of cricket - clearly a man of impeccable taste. As for his death, well, let's just say that he probably went out with a punchline on December 18, 1980.

Toodle-oo!

Allen Ginsberg, the poet who brought us the famous phrase "I saw the best minds of my generation destroyed by madness." Well, I guess we all have our bad days, right? Ginsberg spent his life trying to shock and outrage people with his sexually explicit poetry and political activism. His death was probably just another opportunity for him to make a statement on April 5, 1997.

God bless. Take care of my boy, Roy.

Stan Lee, an American comic book writer and publisher on November 12, 2018.

I came not hither to deny my Lord and Master.

Anne Askew, the English poet and Protestant martyr, had a knack for getting herself into trouble. She was arrested multiple times for her religious beliefs and even dared to challenge the authority of King Henry VIII himself. Her tragic death by burning at the stake was just another reminder that speaking your mind in the 16th century could be a real hot mess. She spoke her last words when offered letter of pardon, before being burned at the stake for heresy on July 16, 1546.

What can it signify?

William Cowper, English poet and hymnodist (25 April 1800), to an attendant who offered him refreshments.

Bring down the curtain, the farce is played out.

François Rabelais, the French writer and Renaissance humanist, was a master of satire and irreverence. His ribald tales of Gargantua and Pantagruel, filled with bawdy humor and scathing social commentary, earned him both admirers and detractors. But even in death, Rabelais kept his wit intact with his final words on March 14, 1553

***Now I'm oiled. Keep me from the rats.**

Pietro Aretino, the notorious Italian author and satirist, was a master of biting
wit and scandalous prose. His writings, filled with raunchy humor and social
critique, earned him both fame and infamy. Even in his final days, Aretino likely
left the world with a smirk on his face, knowing that his sharp pen and scathing
commentary would continue to ruffle feathers long after he was gone. Spoke his final
words on October 21, 1556, after receiving the last rites.

*

To be like Christ is to be a Christian.

William Penn, the founder of Pennsylvania! What a guy. He was born into
wealth and privilege, but that didn't stop him from becoming a Quaker
and preaching about equality and justice. His founding of Pennsylvania was a
masterstroke of PR, too - he convinced people to settle there by claiming it was a land
of milk and honey, conveniently forgetting to mention the cold winters and rocky soil.
Died on July 30, 1718.

John, don't let the awkward squad fire over me.

Robert Burns, the Scottish poet who penned such classic lines as "O my Luve's
like a red, red rose" and "Auld Lang Syne." What a charming fellow he must have
been, traipsing about the Scottish countryside with his quill and ink pot. Of course,
he also had a bit of a reputation as a womanizer, but hey, who doesn't enjoy a good
verse or two about the ladies? As for his death, well, let's just say he enjoyed a bit too
much of the "water of life" and died rather prematurely on July 21, 1796. His last
words was referring to a Dumfries militia to which he belonged.

***Now let her sing and clash, / That glowing sparks may flash! / Morn wakes in
nuptial pride. / Hurrah, thou iron bride! / Hurrah!***

Theodor Körner, German poet and soldier (26 August 1813); final lines of the
"Schwertlied", written two hours before his death in battle.

Clasp my hand, my dear friend, I die!

Vittorio Alfieri, Italian dramatist and poet (8 October 1803), to Princess Louise of Stolberg-Gedern.

I shall not in fact see the new year which I have just commemorated.

Johann Georg Jacobi, German poet (4 January 1814), referring to a poem for New Year's Day that he had completed on New Year's Eve; he in fact lived 5 more days.

I can feel the daisies growing over me.

John Keats, the doomed poet with a penchant for flowers and fairies, penned odes and sonnets with ardor, but his critics saw it as mere "nonsense". His fragile health, romantic escapades, and poetic musings brought little wealth. Alas! His star dimmed too soon, but his verses still bloom, as his fame posthumously grew in magnitude, thanks to his melancholic attitude. Last words spoken on February 23, 1821.

I must sleep now.

Lord Byron, the poet and scandalous rockstar, His life and legacy a wild tale bizarre. With passion and desire, his verses flow, But his death in Greece, a tragic blow. Said his final words before dying during the Greek War of Independence on April 19 , 1824.

Hold your tongue; your wretched style only makes me out of conceit with them.

François de Malherbe, a French poet, critic and translator on October 16, 1628, when listening on his deathbed to his confessor describing the glories of heaven.

I have written nothing which on my deathbed I should wish blotted.

Walter Scott, a Scottish novelist and poet. His life, a mix of fact and fiction. With debts and woes, a financial affliction. Yet, his works endure, his fame so high, Oh, the irony! The bard who made others rich, died nearly nigh on September 21, 1832.

My mind is quite unclouded. I could even be witty.

Coleridge, the dreamer, with a pen so bright. His poems, a wondrous, mind-bending sight. Opium-fueled visions, a creative curse. His life, a haze, a poetic universe. His legacy, a mix of praise and strife. For "Kubla Khan" unfinished, cut short mid-life. The Ancient Mariner, a tale so grim, Coleridge's life and death, a poetic whim until July 25, 1834.

I feel as if I were sitting with Mary at the feet of my Redeemer, hearing the music of his voice, and learning of Him to be meek and lowly.

Felicia Hemans, a poetess refined, Her verses, romantic, with emotions intertwined. With tales of love, grief, and heroic lore, Her life, a delicate dance, a poetic galore until she died on May 16, 1835.

Try to be forgotten. Go live in the country. Stay in mourning for two years, then remarry, but choose somebody decent.

Alexander Pushkin, Russian poet (10 February [O.S. 29 January] 1837), to his wife, Natalia Pushkina, after being mortally wounded in a duel with Georges-Charles de Heeckeren d'Anthès, who was rumored to be having an affair with Natalia.

By the Immortal God, I will not move.

Thomas Love Peacock, English novelist and poet (23 January 1866), fatally burned while trying to save his library from a fire.

My God, my God! Enlighten us. Inspire in a united mankind the love of the good, the love of well being.—To do good, to live for others—that's happiness. Charity, charity, for all the world to be happy. —Widows, small boys—help them.

Pierre-Jean de Béranger, a poet of the street. His rhymes, a biting satire, so sharp and neat. With songs of politics, love, and wine, his life, a revolutionary opus, quite divine. But alas! His death, a somber dirge, his words still echo, a satirical surge. A poet of the people, forever remembered, Béranger's legacy, a satirical flame, still embered. His last words spoken on July 16, 1857.

Now I know that I must be very ill, since you have been sent for.

Henry Wadsworth Longfellow, a master of rhyme, His poems have stood the test of time. The Midnight Ride of Paul Revere was quite grand, But his other works, we don't understand. Last words spoken to his sister on March 24 ,1882.

Why should I not know you, Mary?

Park Benjamin Sr., a scribe with wit and jest. His words, a satire, put readers to the test. A poet and editor, a wordsmith of his time, his life, a literary climb, with puns sublime. Spoke his last words when his wife asked him if he knew her on 12 September 1864.

God bless you! Is that you, Dora?

William Wordsworth, a poet of nature's bliss. His love for landscapes, hard to miss. With daffodils, clouds, and lakes profound, his words, a scenic symphony, so renowned. His life, a wanderer, a poetic quest. Through valleys, hills, and mountains, he was blessed. In solitude, he found poetic inspiration, his verses, a lyrical marvel, a poetic sensation. Wordsworths last words on April 23, 1850 was referring to his daughter, who had died three years earlier.

Holy name!

Charles Baudelaire, the dark poet, a rebel at heart. His life a whirlwind of vice, a provocative art. With poems of debauchery, decadence and woe, his legacy, a scandalous literary show. A dandy in Paris, a bohemian soul, his writings censored, faced society's toll. But his works endure, a controversial treasure, Baudelaire's life and death, a poetic measure since August 31, 1867.

I want to get mumbo-jumbo out of the world.

William Morris, a British textile designer, poet and socialist on October 3, 1896, speaking to his family doctor.

Never mind, I shall soon drink of the river of Eternal Life.

Henry Timrod, the forgotten poet of the Confederacy, lived a life that was anything but glamorous. Despite his literary talent, he struggled to make ends meet and died in obscurity. But fear not, dear reader! His poetry lives on, inspiring generations of Confederate memorabilia collectors and causing high school English teachers everywhere to assign obscure readings. Last words spoken on October 7, 1867. He was unable to swallow a spoonful of water.

Whose house is this? What street are we in? Why did you bring me here? Would you like to see Miss Fairchild?

William Cullen Bryant, a poet quite grand. His words on nature, we can't help but stand. His wit and wisdom, that's what he's known for, but his fashion sense, well, we can't ignore. Black suits and hats, a style quite drab, perhaps he wore them as a mourning hab. Last words spoken on June 12, 1878. He had fallen and hit his head on the sidewalk.

I want to go away.

Alice Cary, the 19th-century poetess with a knack for melancholy verse and a penchant for bonnets, had a tumultuous life. Despite her poetic prowess, she faced poverty and loss, yet persevered with a pen in hand. Her poems brought her fame and fortune, but alas, her epitaph read: "Here lies Alice Cary, with a muse as moody as the weather, whose rhymes now gather dust, but once earned her bread and butter. She died on February 12, 1871.

Then you really think I am dying? At last you think so. But I was right from the first.

Dante Gabriel Rossetti, a painter and poet. His works were praised, no one could oppose it. But his personal life was quite a mess, his love affairs caused him great distress. His artistry was grand, his life a wreck, Perhaps he lost focus of what to protect. Spoke his final words on April 9, 1882.

I must go in, for the fog is rising. (When offered a drink of water.) Oh, is that all it is?

Emily Dickinson, the elusive belle of Amherst. A recluse with a pen and a penchant for dashes. Her poems, like hidden treasures, filled with slant rhymes and enigmatic musings, were discovered posthumously. Yet, her legacy blossomed, and now she's a literary queen, hailed for her wit, wisdom, and poetic routine. Final words before dying on May 15, 1886.

I see such things as you can not dream of.

William Allingham, the poet who penned rhymes with a Victorian flair, lived a life that was the epitome of poetic cliches. From humble beginnings to fame's fleeting grasp, he rhymed of love, nature, and folktales with finesse. But alas, he passed away, his poems still admired, his royalties, nonetheless, expired on November 18, 1889.

I am absolutely undone.

Richard Brinsley Sheridan, an Irish poet, died in poverty on July 7, 1816.

Warry, shift!

Walt Whitman, the good gray poet of America, lived a life that was anything but vanilla. With his unruly beard, free verse, and love of democracy, he penned "Leaves of Grass," a book that shook the literary world. Critics balked, but he persisted, and now he's a national treasure, his beard enshrined, his poems still fresh and refined. Spoke his last words on March 26, 1892 to nurse "Warry" Fritzinger.

I have known thee all the time.

John Greenleaf Whittier, a poet of yore, His words on slavery, let freedom roar. He fought for justice, he fought for right. He spoke his last words when his niece asked if he knew her, on September 7, 1892.

I have opened it.

From the Lady of Shalott to Ulysses bold, his words will forever be told. But his fashion sense, it leaves us in doubt, Ruffled collars and a coat three sizes too stout. **Alfred Lord Tennyson** Died on October 6, 1892.

Don't sole the dead man's shoes yet!

Paul Verlaine, a poet so grand. His works of love and life, we'll understand. But his personal life, oh what a mess, his affair with Rimbaud, it brought him distress. In prison, he wrote nothing great, perhaps his love life sealed his fate. Died on January 8, 1896, after spending much of his later life in poverty.

Hullo.

Is it me you're looking for? No, **Rupert Brooke**, an English poet said his final words to William Denis Browne, who visited him on his deathbed on April 23, 1915.

Valerie.

T. S. Eliot, an American-born British poet on January 4, 1965, whispering the name of his wife, Valerie Eliot.

Goodbye, everybody!

Hart Crane, a poet both bold and bright. Whose words could soar to wondrous heights. With lines that spoke of love and lust, but his life, it was a bit of a bust.. Final words spoken on April 27, 1932, prior to jumping off cruise ship.

Give me the glasses.

Fernando Pessoa, a poet of great pride. Whose words could make one's thoughts collide. With works in languages aplenty, but his personal life, oh what an entity. From multiple personas to drinking with glee, it was a life of mystery for you and me. Last words on November 30, 1935, to the nurse who treated him.

Here Olena Teliha was sitting until she was shot.

With verses that spoke of love and war, but her capture and death, oh what a horror. From her daring activism to her tragic end, Her legacy lives on, it'll never bend. **Olena Telihas** last words an inscription written on the wall of her prison cell prior to her execution by the Gestapo on February 21, 1942.

How sweet it is to rest!

John Taylor, and English poet before his final rest in December 1653.

Yes, but not too many.

Gerrit Achterberg, a poet of great skill. Whose words could give you quite a thrill. With verses that often spoke of death, but his own life, it had a bit of a mess. From murdering his landlady to asylum stays, it's a wonder how he wrote such great phrase. Final words spoken to his companion, who had asked if she should bake some potatoes, on January 17, 1962.

I have something to say to you, sir... 'Tis gone.

Richard Savage, an English poet, before dying on August 1, 1743. He was unable to remember what he wanted to say to his keeper at Bristol Newgate Prison. The keeper found Savage dead the next morning.

I'm going to stop now, but I'm going to sharpen the ax before I put it up, dear.

E.E. Cummings, the avant-garde poet and punctuation rebel, lived a life punctuated by lowercase letters, parentheses, and random line breaks. He wrote poems about love, nature, and the alphabet, earning him a Pulitzer Prize and a cult following of English majors. When he died, the world mourned the loss of a literary iconoclast and a lowercase legend.. Last words on September 3, 1962, to his wife. She was worried it was too hot for him to be chopping wood. He then suffered a stroke.

Philip Larkin. In life, Larkin's words flowed like a lively river, capturing mundane moments with wit and verve. His pen painted portraits of love, lust, and life's absurdity, a bard for the everyday. But alas, Death's grim specter came knocking, and Larkin, with a final poetic flourish, bid adieu to the world, leaving us longing for more of his literary treasure. Last words spoken on December 2, 1985, to his nurse.

Ludovico Ariosto, a poet of knights and dames, with wit and satire, won literary acclaim. But death came calling, and his quill went still on July 6, 1533.

Pierre de Bocosel de Chastelard, a Frenchman of high regard, wrote poetry with passion and flair, but alas, his life was quite rare. He fell in love with Mary, Queen of Scots, but his ardor was met with fraught. He was executed for his treasonous desire, a tragic end to a poet's fire on February 22, 1563. He was addressing the window of Holyrood Palace before being hanged for hiding under the bed of Mary, Queen of Scots.

Paul Scarron, French poet, dramatist and novelist before dying on October 6, 1660.

ANSWERS BEFORE DEATH

On the contrary!

Henrik Ibsen, a playwright renowned. His works acclaimed, his genius profound. From "A Doll's House" to "Peer Gynt" grand, Provoking societal norms, shaking the land. But life's complexities, his soul did wrest, till death's final act, put him to rest. He made his last objection to his maid on May 23, 1906. She had just claimed his health was improving.

I am about the extent of a tenth of a gnat's eyebrow better.

Joel Chandler Harris, a Southern scribe. With Uncle Remus tales, he did imbibe. His Br'er Rabbit stories, a childhood treasure, but his life's quirks, beyond measure. He penned, he charmed, he stirred the pot, untill death knocked, revealing life's twisted plot. Being asked how he felt, Harris knew how to make an impression before dying on July 3, 1908.

I think it is time for morphine.

From Lady Chatterley to Sons and Lovers. His works sparked scandal, minds it covers. Controversial themes, taboo and risqué, but Lawrence's words still resonate today. His life, his words, his fiery breath, Left a literary legacy beyond his death. **D.H Lawrence** spoke his last words just before dying on March 2, 1930. It's always five o'clock somewhere in the world.

Leave the shower curtain on the inside of the tub.

Conrad Hilton, a hotel tycoon grand. Built an empire across the land. With Hilton Hotels, his name renowned. Lavish suites and fine dining abound. No need to comment on the toilet paper. That slip should NEVER EVER face the wall. Hilton stated another obvious answer that annoys people when asked if he had any final words of wisdom before dying on January 3, 1979.

Too late for fruit, too soon for flowers.

Walter de la Mare. A master of the eerie, the strange, and the odd, he captivated readers with his writing prod. But as time passed by, his journey complete. His words still echo, a literary treat. And Walter did find the perfect time to come up with memorable last words! The English author died June 22, 1956, and spoke his final words when asked if he wanted some fruit or flowers.

I feel ill. Call the doctors.

Mao Zedong, leader of the Red. With revolutionary ideas in his head. He rose to power, a communist tide, but his rule brought turmoil far and wide. Great Leap Forward, Cultural Revolution too, his policies, a tragic hullabaloo. Despite his might, his end drew near, Mao passed away, leaving a complex legacy to fear. The Chinese statesman died on September 9, 1976. His rule was responsible for a whooping number of deaths. An estimated 40 to 80 million people perished through persecution, prison labor, starvation, and mass executions. It is not clear if Mao died of karma.

Have I played the part well? Then applaud as I exit!

Augustus, the first Emperor of Rome, was said to have remarked on these words on his deathbed. It's almost like he was doing a final curtain call, as if to say, "I came, I saw, I conquered, and now it's time for my final bow." His legacy as the founder of the Roman Empire remains secure, but at least he went out with a sense of theatrics.

We can, and we've got to, do better than this.

Dr. Seuss, an American children's author, sold over 600 million copies and has been translated into more than 20 languages. His last words before dying on September 24, 1991, have not been translated into much action or copied to a large extent.

With all my heart: I would fain be reconciled to my stomach, which no longer performs its usual functions.

Many wait until their dying breath to bury the hatchet and become reconciled. After all, life is short, and why waste your time building healthy relationships when you can make a grand gesture at the last minute and call it a day? **Charles de Saint-Évremond**, a French soldier and author, opted out of the popular choice and went for a practical one when a clergyman asked if he would be reconciled on September 9, 1703.

I am dying, sir, of a hundred good symptoms.

Alexander Pope, a satirist bold. In verses sharp, his stories told. From "The Rape of the Lock" to "Essay on Man," he mocked society's flawed plan. With wit and sarcasm, he amused. but in death's grasp, he was not amused. His legacy lives on, his words profound, a satirist for ages, still renowned. On being told by his doctor that he was better on the morning of his death on May 30, 1744, the satirist delivered his final masterpiece.

I have not told half of what I saw.

Marco Polo, famed explorer he. Traveled East, across the sea. From Venice to Kublai Khan's court. He chronicled his grand report. Exotic tales of lands unknown, But some said, "Could it all be shown?" Did he exaggerate, they pondered, Or was it all a tale that wandered? Yet Marco Polo's legacy, still captivates in satirical decree. His journeys, stories, and mystique, An enigma that continues to pique. Polo, an explorer, responded to skepticism about the content of his memoir, The Travels of Marco Polo, before dying on January 9, 1324.

Indeed, very good. I shall, have to repeat that, on the Golden Floor.

Housman penned his verse with woe. A melancholic, somber show. From Shropshire lads to heartbreak's sting, he captured sorrow's poignant ring. A poet with a penchant for gloom, Yet his words still echo in each room. Though life was hard, and death was nigh, His poems live on, never to die. **Alfred Edward Housman** said his last words to his doctor, before dying on April 30, 1936. The doctor had just told Housman an edgy joke.

LSD, 100 ug, im

Aldous Huxley, a writer with a wit so sharp. His satires left a lasting mark. Brave New World, his dystopian tale. Predicted a future eerily pale. From drugs to spirituality profound, he explored life's mysteries all around. His legacy, a literary treasure, a satirical voice that brought us pleasure. He tripped out of the world in true colors on November 22, 1963. His last words were a written request to his wife Laura ("im" meaning intramuscular). She obliged. Still, his death was overshadowed, as John F. Kennedy was assassinated hours earlier.

I will, whatever happens.

Johann Strauss, the waltz maestro, so renowned. Melodies enchanting, notes profound. Vienna's favorite son, adored by all, his music made both big and small, Dance with glee, in ballrooms grand. His legacy, a timeless band. In life he swirled, a musical whirl, his melodies continue to unfurl. He finally faced the music on June 3, 1899, and his last words was in response to being asked to get some sleep.

Weary, very weary.

German composer **Felix Mendelssohn**, a musical virtuoso. Composed with flair, a prodigious maestro. From symphonies to oratorios grand, His genius knew no bounds, across the land. But alas, his life cut short, a tragic tale. Leaving a void, a mournful wail. His melodies live on, forever bright. A legacy that shines with musical light. Last words spoken in response to being asked how he felt then fading out on November 4, 1847.

This is the last of Earth. I am content.

John Quincy Adams served as the sixth president of the United States. A true legend in his own mind. Because nothing says "legacy" like being remembered as a mediocre President and a perpetual thorn in the side of his political opponents. He collapsed on the floor of the House of Representatives. Two days later, on February 23, 1848, he passed away in the U.S. Capitol building.

I am still alive!

Caligula, Roman Emperor so infamous. Reign of tyranny, debauchery so shameless. Indulging in excesses, ruthless and bold, madness and cruelty, stories untold. Conquering the land, and loved to be feared. Until a tragic end, by his own guard speared. His rule, a dark chapter in Roman history, a cautionary tale of power's deadly mystery. Known for his madness and extravagance! Some say he even had plans to make his horse a consul. It's a shame he never got to see that dream come true. At least his last words were pretty entertaining. He shouted them before he was stabbed to death by members of the Praetorian Guard on January 24, 41 CE.

Then I die happy.

Epaminondas, general of great acclaim. His military prowess brought him widespread fame. Statesman and strategist, wise and bold. With Thebes' rise, his glory was told. But, in battle, he met his tragic end. Leaving Thebes to mourn a fallen friend. A legend in history, his legacy stands. As a brilliant tactician in ancient lands. He pulled out the weapon with which he had been impaled in battle once he heard the enemy was fleeing on 362 BCE.

Bad.

Hans von Bülow, a maestro of the keys. A virtuoso known for his musical expertise. Married to Liszt's daughter, a union profound. But love's sweet melodies soon lost their sound. Divorced and embittered. he led a life of strife, till death's final chord ended his tumultuous life. His last word was in response to being asked how he felt before dying on February 12, 1894.

I don't want it.

Marie Curie, a pioneer of science renowned. With intellect and courage, she was crowned. Her quest for knowledge knew no bounds. Her discoveries brought laurels, and world-renowned. Her work with radium and polonium bright, untill death took her in its cold and unforgiving might. She won the Nobel Prize in two different fields of science. Probably one of the smartest people ever lived, the scientist had this answer upon being offered a painkilling injection on July 4 1934.

The meager satisfaction that man can extract from reality leaves him starving.

Sigmund Freud, the father of psychoanalysis bold. Unraveled the mysteries of the human mind, we're told. With dreams and desires, he delved deep. Explored the unconscious with methods unique. But in the end, he succumbed to life's final fate, his legacy, however, continues to fascinate. Freud digged deep and delivered his final answer before dying on September 23, 1939.

I want to go when I want. It is tasteless to prolong life artificially. I have done my share, it is time to go. I will do it elegantly.

Albert Einstein, a genius beyond compare, E=mc^2, a formula rare. His theories shook the world of physics to its core. A Nobel laureate, admired galore. But as time went on, his hair turned gray, and he left this world in a cosmic way, declining surgery the day before his death on April 18, 1955.

Far from well, yet far better than mine iniquities deserve.

Richard Mather, a Puritan divine. Preached fire and brimstone, a stern design. A scholar and preacher, devout and severe. With sermons that struck terror and fear. He guided his flock with a rigid hand, until he passed to the heavenly land on April 22, 1669.

*So much the better. I am happy that I shall not live to see the surrender of Quebec.
I have much business that must be attended to of greater moment than your
ruined garrison and this wretched country.*

Montcalm, a Frenchman of noble breed. Fought wars with honor, a valiant deed.
He led his troops with skill and might, but, defeat was his final sight. In battle's
fray, he met his fate, a hero remembered, a gallant state. His last words on being told
the wound he had received at the Battle of the Plains of Abraham was mortal on
September 14, 1759.

The worse, the better for me.

Edward Alderson, the judge so stern and wise. Rendered verdicts that took some
by surprise. His legal acumen, sharp and keen, made him feared in courts, a legal
machine. But life is fleeting, death comes to all, even judges must answer the final
call. Now he rests, his gavel laid to rest, a witty judge, among the legal best. Last words
spoken when asked how he felt on January 27, 1857.

*Relieved to hear that you feel better. I had a very bad night—am now stronger.
Your poor Louis.*

Ludwig von Benedek, a military strategist. With plans so grand and tactics so
brisk. In battles fought, his glory was told, his strategies bold, or so we were told.
But war's uncertain fortunes, oh so cruel. Turned the tide and proved him a fool. In
defeat, he fell from grace, his military prowess lost its place. Now remembered in
history's pages, as a general with well-intentioned rages. Last words written to his wife
on April 27, 1881.

O, better.

Robert G. Ingersoll, a lawyer bold and bright. Debating religion day and night.
His wit and logic held the floor, as he challenged dogmas to the core. But alas, his
final case was won, and now he rests, his battle done. Leaving a legacy, free thought's
voice, forever echoing, a reason-filled rejoice. Last words to his wife when she asked
him how he felt on July 21, 1899.

Mind your business!

Wyndham Lewis, a man of arts. Both written words and painted parts. His works avant-garde, his style unique, critics praised, while some did sneer and critique. A life well-lived, a creative flame, but now extinguished, though he leaves a lasting name. In words and strokes, his legacy lives on, a satirical visionary, long after he's gone. Final words spoken when asked on his deathbed about his bowels on March 7, 1957.

No.... Awfully jolly of you to suggest it, though.

Ronald Knox, a cleric bold and bright. A writer known for his wit and insight. With pen and pulpit, he preached the truth, but satire, too, was in his youth. A man of faith, both wise and sly, he penned his tales with a gleam in his eye. Now laid to rest, his words still linger, a literary memento, with a heavenly zinger. Final words when Lady Elton asked if he would like her to read from his translation of the New Testament on August 24, 1957.

Of course I know who you are. You're my girl. I love you.

John Wayne, the cowboy king. On screen he'd ride, shoot, and sing. With swagger and drawl, he'd play his part, a rugged hero with a cowboy heart. But, his curtain call did come, a legend remembered, a life well-done. Now in celluloid forever enshrined, a western icon, one of a kind. Last words spoken to his daughter, Aissa Wayne, who had asked if he knew who she was on June 11, 1979.

No, I don't believe so.

Rock Hudson, the heartthrob star. With charm and looks that went so far. A dazzling smile, a voice so smooth, in films and shows he'd always groove. But life's cruel twist, a shocking blow, Hudson's secret, the world didn't know, A closeted gay, afraid to be free, Hollywood's facade, his tragedy. Rumors spread, whispers abound, Tinseltown's hypocrisy profound, Hudson's demise, a hush affair. Covered up with utmost care. The AIDS epidemic, a deadly storm, Claimed Hudson's life, a tragic norm, on October 2, 1985.

My Florida water.

Lucy, the queen of TV delight. Her antics brought laughter every night. From "I Love Lucy" to "The Lucy Show", she ruled the small screen, stealing the show. A shrewd businesswoman, sharp and sly. With a keen eye for a TV buy, she produced shows, built her own empire, a sitcom legend who'd never tire. But fame and fortune couldn't fend, off time's cruel march, it'd always send. Her final bow, a curtain call, Left us mourning the loss of funny **Lucille Ball**. Final words spoken when asked if she wanted anything on April 26, 1989.

Extremely well, and as became the descendant of so many kings.

Charmion. Cleopatra's devoted aide. Loyal to the end, poison she obeyed. A tragic fate, a faithful slave, forever remembered for the role she gave. Last words spoken when one of Emperor Augustus' men asked her, "Was this well done of your lady, Charmion?" She then died on August 12, 30 BCE.

Under the feet of my friars.

Saint Dominic, a priest so divine. Founded the Dominicans, a holy sign. With zeal and faith, he preached the Word, converting souls, a mission he spurred. His order grew, spreading wide, preaching truth with religious pride. But now, his saintly story's told, leaving behind a legacy, precious as gold. Last words spoken when asked where he wanted to be buried on August 6, 1221.

I have already confessed my sins to God.

Franz von Sickingen, a knight so bold. Fought for reform, the truth he told. Against the Church's grip, he rebelled. A Protestant leader, fear he quelled. But battles lost, his fortune waned, injured, defeated, his cause strained. His crusade ended, his dreams denied, Franz von Sickingen, a fallen knight, he died. Final words when his chaplain asked if he wanted to confess prior to his death defending his castle on May 7, 1523.

Philip Melanchthon, a reformer bright. Luther's ally, his intellectual might. With pen and wit, he penned treatises strong. Challenging the Church, righting the wrong. His teachings spread, his influence grand. A scholar's mind; a theologian's hand. But, his days, they came to an end. Leaving behind a legacy, a reformer's friend. Final words spoken on April 19, 1560, when asked if he wanted anything.

Absolutely, and I pray God to condemn me, if I have had any other aim than the welfare of God and the state.

Cardinal Richelieu, a cunning Cardinal. Played power games, political and tactical. A master manipulator, a political mind. His influence and ambition, hard to find. As France's ruler, he held the reins. Controlling the monarchy with strategic gains. But in death's embrace, he met his fate. A legacy of power, love or hate? Debate! Final words spoken on his deathbed on December 4, 1642, when asked whether he pardoned his enemies.

Bad, bad! To judge by what I now endure, the hand of death grasps me sharply.

Salvator Rosa, a talent unique. Art and poetry, his creative technique. Rebellious and bold, his works avant-garde. Challenging norms, pushing art's regard. But life's struggles, they took their toll. Rosa's genius, a troubled soul. In death, his art still captivates. A legacy ironic, a master who frustrates. Final words spoken when asked how he was on March 15, 1673.

I want nothing but death.

Jane Austen, a literary gem. Her novels, cherished, a timeless stem. With wit and humor, she spun her tales. Entertaining readers with romantic trails. From Elizabeth Bennet to Emma Woodhouse, her characters brought charm to every house. But, her life was cut too short, leaving behind a legacy, a literary fort. Last words when being asked by her sister Cassandra if she wanted something on July 18, 1817.

Go, your countrymen need you. For me, there is now no more you can do.

Christina Petronella, a vivacious soul. A life of adventure, her ultimate goal. From daring escapades to travels grand, her tales of excitement, they would expand. But fate had other plans, a sudden end. Leaving memories cherished, to forever fend. Her spirit lives on, in stories told, a life well-lived, a legend to behold. Spoke her final words to her husband, Voortrekker leader Andries Pretorius, who had been asked to lead the Boers at the Battle of Boomplaats in September, 1848.

Nothing, only 'love one another'.

William H. Seward, a statesman renowned. With diplomacy and skill, he astound. As Secretary of State, he played his part, negotiating deals with a savvy heart. From the Alaska purchase to foreign affairs, he faced challenges with strategic cares. But sadly, his time on earth was through, leaving a legacy, a diplomat true. Last words on October 10, 1872, when asked if he had any final words.

Yes, my dear Robert, you are.

Marcel Proust, a writer profound. With introspection, his tales abound. In search of lost time, he delved deep, unraveling memories, in language steep. His words painted worlds, rich and vast, a literary maestro, unsurpassed. But as life goes on, time takes its toll, leaving behind a legacy, a literary soul. Final words spoken on November 18, 1922 to his brother, who asked if he was hurting him.

No.

Alfred Rosenberg, a man of power. With ideology sold, a leader's tower. A key figure in a dark regime, spreading propaganda, a twisted theme. But in the end, his fortunes fell, a legacy tainted, a bitter spell. History's lessons, a cautionary tale, of a life and death, that did bewail. Rosenberg was executed 16 October 1946 for war crimes and crimes against humanity. The German was the only condemned nazi at the Nuremberg trials who, when asked at the gallows if he had any last statement to make, replied with only one words.

When You Know You Are Dying

I am about to—or I am going to—die; either expression is correct.

Dominique Bouhours, a French priest and grammarian. He secured his legacy on May 27, 1702.

I regret that I should leave this world without again beholding him.

Presiding over the so-called "Era of Good Feelings," which was marked by one-party rule and a general lack of political opposition, **James Monroe**, the fifth president of the United States, passed away five years to the date after his fellow Founding Fathers, Adams, and Jefferson, on July 4. Not regretting much, his last words referencing his close friend, the fourth president of the United States, fellow Founding Father James Madison.

I am dying. Please... bring me a toothpick.

Alfred Jarry, a French writer, died with impeccable teeth on November 1, 1907.

I am ill, very ill. I shall not recover.

John Lothrop Motley was an American author and historian making history on May 29, 1877.

I did not answer the letters of my friends because I could not write, as no sooner did I take a pen in my hand than I felt as if I was dying.

English poet **Edward Lear** possibly died of writer's block in the arteries on January 29, 1888.

I shall have to ask leave to desist, when I am interrupted by so great an experiment as dying.

William **Davenant**, an English poet setting aside the manuscript of a new poem before passing away April 7, 1668.

Give me! Give me! Come on, give me! The ladder! Quick, pass me the ladder!

Nikolai **Gogol** was a Russian author of Ukrainian origin (like all "Russian" writers, don´t be confused when googling Gogol"). Uncertain if he needed to climb out of hell or up to heaven as he uttered these words in his dying moments on March 4, 1852.

I know what you are thinking of, but I have nothing to communicate on the subject of religion.

Mary **Wollstonecraft**, an English writer, died on September 10, 1797, after giving birth to the mother of Frankenstein, Mary Shelley.

I die for my homeland.

Francisco **Solano López**, the former President of Paraguay, left behind a legacy as disastrous as his military strategies. He led his country into a devastating war that resulted in the deaths of most of Paraguay's population and the destruction of its economy. At least he had a really cool mustache when he was killed in battle on March 1, 1870, during the Paraguayan War.

It is likely you may never need to do it again.

Scottish poet **James Hogg** asked his wife to watch by his bedside before dying on November 21, 1835. He was right, leaving this world with memorable literature and not so interesting final last words.

I am imploring you. Burn all the indecent poems and drawings.

English illustrator and author **Aubrey Beardsley**. Possibly foreseen the woke age of the internet on March 16, 1898. 68 years later, officials charged a gallery owner who exhibited Beardsley´s work under obscenity laws.

I hope to meet each of you in heaven. Be good, children, all of you, and strive to be ready when the change comes.

Andrew **Jackson** was the seventh president of the United States and died on June 8, 1845. Jackson and his spouse, Rachel Donelson, had no children together. Unclear what children he spoke of, but some children might be excluded. He perpetrated genocide against Native American tribes and defied the Supreme Court in the name of expanding American territory.

What are you doing, comrades? I am yours and you are mine!

Galba's rule, a miser's stingy spree, Empty coffers, Rome's misery, Legacy brief, a forgettable tale, Death swift, a coup, end of his failed trail. His reign came to an end when he was killed by the Praetorians on January 15, 69 AD.

Now I die.

Joseph **Blanco White**, a Spanish poet, stated the obvious on May 20, 1841.

Doctor, I am going. Perhaps it is best.

John Tyler, the 10th President of the United States, is a true role model for aspiring politicians everywhere. He taught us that the best way to win friends and influence people is by switching political parties mid-term, getting kicked out of your own party, and having the entire country forget you were ever President in the first place. He died on January 18, 1862, aged 71.

Tomorrow, at sunrise, I shall no longer be here.

Ah, **Nostradamus**, the great soothsayer! Who saw the future, or was he a player? His prophecies were known far and wide. Predicting wars, disasters, and the tide. But some say his words were vague and unclear. And hard to interpret, year after year. Did he really foresee all that he claimed, or was it just guesswork, all the same? Perhaps his words were just a lucky guess, and we give him too much credit, nothing less. Yet still we marvel at his foresight, and wonder if his predictions were right. However, in 1566 he was deadly accurate on one little thing, predicting July 2 as the dying day of the seer King. Maybe not so strange, he was very ill. Nonetheless, it gives people a thrill.

**Whistling*

Irish author **Patrick Pearse** did not say anything but whistled on his way to execution by firing squad on May 3, 1916. I have the "Bridge on the River Kwai" theme in my head now. No sources can confirm this is what he whistled. But it could be because "Colonel Bogey March" was composed in 1914. Sorry if I put that damned whistled theme in your brain.

If I die, bury me up there [in the churchyard at Roquebrune], and then in a year's time, when the newspapers have forgotten me, dig me up and plant me in Sligo.

W.B. **Yeats**, an Irish poet, was buried in Roquebrune after his death on January 28, 1939. Nine years later, bones were sent from Roquebrune to Sligo and buried. However, it turns out bones from another person were sent. Be careful what you wish for.

Zachary Taylor, the 12th President of the United States, left behind a legacy as memorable as his facial hair. Known for his uneventful presidency and lack of political experience, he proved that sometimes, the best qualifications for the job are a catchy campaign slogan and a good mustache. He died in office on July 9 1850, after serving only 16 months in office.

Cotton Mather, a pious divine, Puritan preacher, righteousness did shine. Witch trials, smallpox, his claims renowned, But superstition, his wisdom confound. Legacy mixed, a complex array, intellects clashed, in a zealous fray. Famed author, yet controversy rife, in death, his dogma, a fading life. His wife wiped his eyes with her handkerchief as he said the last words, alluding to Revelation 21:4, on February 13, 1728.

He could be called the first ever Bad Boy in literature after he established the bad boys book subgenre with the semi-autobiographical The Story of a Bad Boy. However **Thomas Bailey Aldrich**, an American author and editor dying on March 19, 1907. However it was really his wife, Lilian Woodman, who was a bad … glitch. In Mark Twains words; "Lord, I loathe that woman so! She is an idiot—an absolute idiot—and does not know it … and her husband, the sincerest man that walks … tied for life to this vacant hellion, this clothes-rack, this twaddling, blethering, driveling blatherskite!»

Paolo Farinati, Italian Mannerist painter, on his deathbed in 1606. His wife replied, "I will bear you company, my dear husband," and also died.

If you wish for another cheerful evening with your old friend, there is no time to be lost.

Mary Russell Mitford, words her art. Her rustic tales, won readers' heart. Country life, her muse and theme, but fame and wealth, a distant dream. Her legacy, a quaint pastoral scene, her stories cherished, like a rare cuisine. Yet critics scoffed, at her rustic pen, a satirical life, till the very end. Mitford died after being involved in a dramatic carriage accident on January 10, 1855.

Oh, do not cry. Be good children, and we shall meet in heaven.

Andrew Johnson, the 17th President of the United States, left behind a legacy as divisive as his impeachment trial. He had the honor of being the first President to be impeached, but somehow managed to avoid being removed from office. His legacy includes undoing much of the progress made during Reconstruction and inspiring countless angry rants from history buffs. Boringly, he almost replicated Andrew Jackson's last words when he died on July 31, 1875.

I have lost the day!

He sure lost it that day, **Titus**. A Roman emperor who ruled from 79 until he died 13 september 81 CE. His last words are not known with certainty, a few different versions have been passed down through the ages. One account suggests that Titus said, "I have made but one mistake." However, the mistake he was referring to is not known. He was regarded as a successful ruler. During his reign, he oversaw the completion of many important construction, including the rubble known as the Colosseum.

No, but comfortable enough to die.

Maria Theresa, empire's matriarch, Reforms bold, a monarch's march, Legacy bright, a reign of power, Austria's queen, in history's tower. This was her reply when her son said, "Your Majesty cannot be comfortable like that» on November 29, 1780.

Mary Blandy, a tragic tale. A murder charge, a scandalous wail. Her father's poison, her deadly hand. A crime of passion, a dark demand. Her legacy, a cautionary fright. Crime doesn't pay, in the moral light. Her fame, a tale of murderous dread. Mary Blandy, left the world with bloodshed. Spoke her last words on April 6, 1752, prior to execution by hanging.

François-Jean, aristocratic blunder. A freethinker's mind, a social thunder. Mocked religion, society's norm. Landed in jail, a blasphemous storm. His legacy, a martyr for free thought, his fate, a lesson, for those who fought. Against dogma, intolerance's sting, François-Jean, a rebel, with a tragic ending. Spoken on July 1, 1766, prior to execution by beheading for blasphemy and sacrilege.

Emanuel Swedenborg, a curious mind. Theology, science, mysticism entwined. A polymath's pursuit, a cosmic quest. Divine visions, put his faith to the test. His legacy, a man of many realms, a mystic's musings, both science and helms. Controversial figure, revered and mocked, Swedenborg's legacy, a puzzle locked. Spoken before he clocked out on March 29, 1772.

Joseph Warren, doctor with a cause. A patriot's heart, fighting for laws. Revolutionary leader, voice so loud, Champion of freedom, brave and proud. His legacy, a hero's tale, fighting for independence, without fail. His death, a martyr's sacrifice, Joseph Warren, a patriot's demise. Warren was mortally wounded at the Battle of Bunker Hill and died on June 17, 1775.

I only regret that I have but one life to give for my country.

Nathan Hale, a spy so bold. In Revolutionary times, he was told. To gather intel, for his nation's might, but caught by the Brits, a perilous plight. His legacy, a symbol of sacrifice, a patriot's courage, beyond a price. "Hanged as a spy," his epitaph read, Nathan Hale, a hero, even in death's dread. Final words on September 22, 1776, before being hanged by the British for his involvement in the American Revolutionary War.

I feel sleepy, a short time of rest would do me good.

Gustav III, a regal showman. King of Sweden, with a royal plan. A patron of arts, a man of flair, but enemies plotted, with a deadly snare. Assassinated in a masked ball's haze, a monarch's fate, in a tragic craze. His legacy, a king who left a mark, Gustav III, a ruler, both bright and dark. He spoke his final words in a hospital bed on March 29, 1792, after being shot at a masquerade two weeks earlier.

I am dying; leave me alone.

Johann Georg Ritter von Zimmermann, a polymath rare. Swiss writer, with knowledge to spare. Philosopher, naturalist, and physician, a Renaissance man, with boundless ambition. His legacy, a tome of learned lore, A treasure trove of wisdom galore, but fame eluded, his name obscured, Johann Georg, a polymath, less procured. Last words before dying on October 7, 1795.

I have not yet lost my feeling for humanity.

Immanuel Kant, a thinker profound. Philosopher extraordinaire, world-renowned. Categorical imperatives, ethics his creed. Critique of Pure Reason, his mighty seed. His legacy, philosophical might, a moral compass, shining bright. Though departed, his ideas endure, Immanuel Kant, a thinker pure. Kant was thanking his physicians and attendants with his final words on February 12, 1804.

I shall not live more than two days, therefore make haste.

William Woodville, physician keen. With herbs and plants, a botanical dream. Curing ailments, with medicinal flair, botanical remedies, beyond compare. His legacy, a contribution profound, to botany's world, knowledge renowned, Though he has left, his work lives on, William Woodville, a botanist, now long gone. Final words spoken on March 26, 1805 to a carpenter he had summoned to measure him for his coffin.

Let's go, this will be for the last time.

Sophie Blanchard, a daring soul. Soared the skies, her fame did roll. As aeronaut extraordinaire, her flights, a thrilling affair. Her legacy, a pioneering feat, conquering heights, in a balloon's seat. But, a tragic end one day, Sophie Blanchard, aeronaut's final display. She spoke her last words on July 6, 1819 prior to lighting fireworks that ignited the gas in her balloon, causing it to crash and Blanchard to fall to her death.

I am a dead man! Lord, have mercy upon me!

Gaston III, Count of Foix, a nobleman bold. Warrior skilled, with stories untold. His legacy, battles fought and won, a champion of Foix, under the sun. But fate had other plans in store, death's hand, a tragic lore, Gaston III, now laid to rest, a legend remembered, among the best. Last known words said before dying in 1391.

Nostitz, you have learned many a thing from me. Now you are to learn how peacefully a man can die.

Gebhard Leberecht von Blücher, a military man. Prussian field marshal, with a cunning plan. He led his troops with fiery might, in battles fierce, a formidable sight. His legacy, victories renowned, a hero on the battleground. But, his time did end, leaving behind a military legend, my friend. Final words on September 12, 1819 to his aide-de-camp, August Ludwig von Nostitz.

I feel quite well, only very weak.

Ann Hasseltine Judson, a missionary bold. Traveled afar, spreading the faith she extolled. Her legacy, a tireless quest, to save souls, in lands far west. But fate was cruel, her life cut short, leaving behind a legacy, a heavenly report. Ann Hasseltine Judson, a missionary's fate. Her work remembered, beyond her earthly state. Last words before dying of smallpox in Amherst, Burma on October 24, 1826.

Thank you—but don't kiss me; it is the sweat of death. I am dying, and it's for the best.

John Field, a pianist grand. Played his keys with skilled command. Legacy of melodies sweet, with piano pieces, a virtuoso's feat. His compositions, a musical delight, a maestro's touch, with notes so bright. But, his final bow was made, leaving behind a musical accolade. Last words spoken on January 23, 1837 to his friend Gebhard.

Now I am about to take my last voyage, a great leap in the dark.

Thomas Hobbes, a mind profound, his philosophies oft renowned. With "Leviathan" as his creed, power, politics, his scholarly seed. Yet critics scoffed, and foes did jest, as Hobbes' ideas were put to the test. His legacy debated, his views dissected, but his philosophical impact never neglected. Spoke his final words on December 4, 1679.

I am about to leave you. I have labored in the sanctuary fifty-three years, and this is my comfort and confidence, that I have never labored without blood in the vessel. Goodbye! Drive on!

Christmas Evans, a preacher bold. His sermons fiery, tales untold. Legacy of fervent faith. With nonconformity as his wraith. From humble beginnings, he did rise, proclaiming gospel to the skies. His life's work, a minister's quest, leaving behind a spiritual zest since dying on July 19, 1838.

I am ready—let there be no mistake and no delay.

Robert Blum, a man of zeal. With democratic dreams surreal. Fighting for the people's rights, through tumultuous, revolutionary nights. But foes were fierce, resistance stout, Blum's legacy clouded with doubt. His death a martyr's tragic fate, a symbol of change, albeit late. Blum spoke his last words on November 9, 1848 prior to execution by firing squad.

Not yet.

Frédéric Chopin's keys, a melodic dance. His piano prowess, a grand romance. Polish pride, talent renowned, but coughing fits left him unsound. A legacy of music divine, a genius at the ivories, so fine. His death, a tragic end to his tale, but his melodies forever prevail. Gave his final answer on October 17, 1849, when asked by his physician if he was suffering.

I am weary; I will now go to sleep. Good night!

Neander, the theologian bold and wise. With church history, he'd analyze. A legacy of scholarship grand, but often misunderstood in his land. His works, a treasure trove of knowledge. Yet some found him too rigid, lacked his college. In death, his legacy shines bright, his insights still guide us with scholarly light. Final words on July 14, 1850.

No, Your Majesty, tomorrow you will not see me here.

Camillo Benso, Count of Cavour, the statesman with a cunning plan. Unifying Italy, he took a bold stand. A legacy of politics and finesse, with diplomacy, he cleaned up the mess. Prime Minister, skilled in the art of intrigue, bringing states together in a political league. His death left a nation in mourning, but his legacy lives on, Italy's fate transforming. Last words on June 6, 1861 to Victor Emmanuel II of Italy, who had said he would see him tomorrow.

I might have lived another year if I had not caught this cold, but I am satisfied to go now. I am eighty-four years old—long past the allotted time of man—and at my age, life becomes a burden.

William Backhouse Astor Sr., the tycoon of wealth so grand. With riches vast at his command. Built fortunes with shrewd acumen, a legacy admired by many men. But greed and wealth, a fickle friend. Could not stave off life's bitter end. For death's embrace, it knows no bounds, even for the richest man around when he died on November 24, 1875).

And now I am officially dead.

Abram Hewitt, United States Congressman and Mayor of New York City, removing his oxygen mask and stating the obvious ever since January 18, 1903.

This time it will serve me for the voyage from which there is no return, the voyage of eternity.

Claude Bernard, a renowned physiologist, pushed the boundaries of scientific inquiry with his pioneering experiments. His findings on the inner workings of the body earned him the title of "Master of the Lab." But alas, even a master cannot outrun the Grim Reaper, who brought Claude's research to a sudden halt. Though gone on February 10, 1878, his legacy lives on, reminding us all that life's lab experiments often end in an unexpected conclusion. Cheers to you, Claude, for your scientific "je ne sais quoi»!

I am not in the least afraid to die.

Charles Darwin, the man who shook the world with his theory of evolution, caused quite the commotion among the pious. His "Origin of Species" had creationists in a tizzy, but Chuck stood firm, flaunting his finches. Alas, old Charlie took his final voyage on April 19, 1882.

I feel very badly.

Richard Wagner, the operatic maestro, composed epics that stretched for hours on end, testing the bladders of even the most devoted fans. His Wagnerian saga lives on, a symphony of controversy and drama. Though his music still stirs souls, old Richard's final curtain call on February 13, 1883 was more dramatic than his most famous librettos.

At rest at last. Now I am free from pain.

Thomas A. Hendricks, Vice President supreme, served the nation with an air of obscurity. His legacy? Uhm...let's see. Oh yes, he was a Vice President, right? In life and death, he remained a footnote in the annals of U.S. history, the VP who kept us guessing. But he is free from pain since November 25, 1885.

Enough, Enough.

Fred C. Roberts, the medical maverick, braved jungles and deserts in his quest to heal the ailing. With his trusty stethoscope and sense of adventure, he brought medicine to the far reaches of the world. His legacy lives on, a tale of daring deeds and bedside manners. Spoke his last words on June 6, 1894, dying in Tientsin, China.

How good!

Alexander III, the czar so tough, with his bejeweled scepter and shiny cuff. He ruled with an iron hand, crushed rebellion with a stern command. But alas, life can be unkind, and fate had its way. His rule cut short, the curtain fell, ending Alexander's royal play. All hail the czar, who left his mark, a tale of power, intrigue, and a monarchy in the dark! On November 1, 1894, he spoke his final words when the priest placed his hands on his head after performing the last rites as he died.

Here I go. Here I go. Here I go.

Cromwell Dixon, a high-flying maverick, took to the skies, making history iconic. His aviation feats were quite the sensation, soaring above with youthful elation. But, his flight was short-lived, a sudden twist, fate's cruel gift. Cromwell's legacy, a pioneer's dream, a soaring spirit, forever in flight it seems! Spoke his final words as his biplane crashed sideways on October 2, 1911.

It is nothing... it is nothing...

Archduke Franz Ferdinand, a royal heir, had a penchant for travel, without a care. His fateful trip to Sarajevo turned askew, as an assassin's bullet pierced him through. A single shot, a world ablaze, Franz's legacy, a catalyst in history's maze. A royal tragedy, that changed the world's fate, oh dear Franz, history's unpredictable twist of late! Spoke his last words after being fatally shot by 19-year-old Gavrilo Princip on June 28, 1914.

I would give anything just to have written this.

Richard Strauss, the musical maverick, composed symphonies both grand and dramatic. His operas wowed the crowd, but sometimes left them feeling wowed-out. Yet, his baton waved with skill and finesse, until his final note, a mournful caress. Strauss, the maestro, a legend in his right, may his music continue to shine bright! Strauss was holding a copy of Mozart's Clarinet Concerto when he spoke his last words on September 8, 1949.

As you see, I am crying too, not tears of pain but tears of joy, because I'll be with my God in a short time.

Emil Kapaun, the chaplain brave, marched with troops, souls to save. In war's chaos, he brought solace and prayer, lifting spirits with pastoral care. His Medal of Honor, a testament to his devotion, a hero in faith, with unwavering emotion. Kapaun's legacy, a saintly lore, a soldier's guardian, forevermore. Spoke his last words before dying in prisoner of war camp on May 23, 1951 during the Korean War.

No. Thanks for everything.

Max Beerbohm, the master of wit, penned essays that would so often hit. His parodies and caricatures, oh so clever, mocking society's flaws, endeavor after endeavor. With his pen, he drew and wrote with flair, a satirical genius, beyond compare. On being asked by his wife if he had had a good sleep, he said his final words on May 20, 1956.

Nothing matters. Nothing matters.

Louis B. Mayer, a mogul in the showbiz game, made movies that brought him fortune and fame. His studio's stars shone bright, but behind the scenes, a tyrant's might. The golden era's kingpin, a Hollywood maven, but his legacy marred by scandals, his reputation shaken. Mayer's final scene, a curtain drawn, a Hollywood titan, now forever gone. Final words spoken on October 29, 1957.

If this is death, then I am ready for it.

Billy Whelan, the football ace, with skills that left opponents in a daze. He dribbled, he scored, he thrilled the crowd, his talent loud and clear, never allowed. But fate played a cruel hand, cut short his plight, Whelan's legacy, a football legend's eternal light. Spoke his last words during British European Airways Flight 609's third takeoff attempt prior to the Munich air disaster, on February 6, 1958.

Dying is easy. Comedy is difficult.

Edmund Gwenn, the actor jolly, brought cheer to screens, both big and small-y. With a twinkle in his eye and a rosy cheek, he charmed audiences, week after week. From Kris Kringle in "Miracle on 34th Street," a holiday delight, to other roles, pure acting might. Gwenn's legacy, a talent so fine, a thespian treasure, for all of time. Alas, he bid adieu, the final act, but his performances, forever intact. Last words spoken before dying on September 6, 1959.

I've had a hell of a lot of fun and I've enjoyed every minute of it.

Errol Flynn, a dashing star, with looks that could take you quite far. From swashbuckling adventures to leading man roles, he captivated audiences with his daring roles. Off-screen antics, a wild escapade, scandals and drama, never did fade. Flynn's legacy, a Hollywood tale, a charming rogue, a legend's sail. But, his final act was played, a life lived bold, a legacy made. Final words spoken before dying on October 14, 1959.

I'm bored with it all.

Winston Churchill, a British bulldog true, with a cigar and a whiskey brew. He led the war, with speeches grand, inspiring the nation, across the land. But witty remarks and a quick retort, sometimes caused a political sport. A statesman bold, a legend renowned, Churchill's legacy, forever renowned. Though he's gone, his spirit lives on, in history's pages, a leader long drawn. Las words before dying on January 24, 1965.

I'd rather be skiing than doing this. (When asked if he skied). No, but I'd rather be doing that than doing this.

Stan Laurel, English actor, member of the duo Laurel and Hardy. Last words spoken to a nurse on February 23, 1965.

You see, this is how you die.

Coco Chanel, a fashion queen, with style and flair, the industry's sheen. Her little black dress, a timeless hit, her fragrance, a scent that would truly fit. From humble roots, she rose up high, with her designs, she ruled the sky. But life's drama, a turbulent ride, Coco Chanel, fashion's bold guide. Her legacy lives, her name renowned, her fashion empire, forever crowned. To her maid as she died in fashion on January 10, 1971.

Oh, to die in Italy!

John Carradine, a thespian great. with roles diverse, from love to hate. His booming voice, a commanding tone, on stage and screen, he'd hold his own. From horror flicks to westerns grand, Carradine's talent, always in demand. Though he's gone, his films remain, a legacy of an actor's reign. Spoken on November 27, 1988, dying in Milan, Italy.

Don't worry. Relax.

Rajiv Gandhi's life, a meteoric rise, From Prime Minister's seat to tragic demise. With youth and charm, he won the hearts, But fate had a bomb, that tore him apart. Las words spoken to a policewoman at his assassination on May 21, 1991.

I'm going to be with Gloria now.

James Stewart, the iconic star, From "It's a Wonderful Life" to "Mr. Smith," he went far. With his drawl and charm, he won our hearts, But heaven called him with its cinematic arts on July 2, 1997.

You're right. It's time. I love you all.

Michael Landon, the TV heartthrob. With his boyish looks, he had the mob. From "Bonanza" to "Little House," he made us swoon. But cancer came knocking, way too soon. Hollywood's sweetheart, a star so bright. But life's script had a tragic plight. With tears and tissues, we said goodbye, as "Highway to Heaven" reached the sky. Last words on July 1, 1991 when one of his sons said it was time to move on.

Forgive me, but I don't want to live anymore. The pain is too bad. There's no point in trying to prolong this agony.

Brian Keith, the actor so dandy. From "Family Affair" to "The Chisholms," just grand andy. A career on screen, with talent so bright. But life's end, a curtain call, a somber night. Last words spoken to his wife Victoria before dying on June 24, 1997.

I'm losing it.

Frank Sinatra, the Chairman of the Board. With his voice so smooth, he struck a chord. From "My Way" to "New York, New York," he sang, But his offstage antics, a scandalous bang. A swinging lifestyle, with mobster ties, Romantic escapades, that reached the skies. But time caught up, as years went by, a legend's farewell, with a final sigh on May 14, 1998.

Leave me alone, I'm fine.

Barry White, the soulful crooner. With his deep voice, a seductive tuner. From "Can't Get Enough of Your Love, Babe" to "You're the First, the Last, My Everything", his music set the mood, like a romantic fling. A lover's anthem, a disco groove, But his love life, a tempestuous move. With marriages and divorces, a tumultuous ride, A heartbreak ballad, a love-sick bride. Left his earthly stage and spoke his final words to a nurse on July 4, 2003.

I'm dying.

Steve Irwin, the Crocodile Hunter bold. With his khaki shorts and antics told. From wrestling crocs to saving snakes. His passion for wildlife, no one could shake. But one fateful sting, a tragic blow, a stingray's venom, a deadly show. A conservationist's irony, cruel and bizarre. The wildlife warrior, lost to nature's scar on September 4, 2006.

I guess my flying days are over.

Johnny Miller, an American aviation pioneer spoke his last words, to his nephew while dying at the age of 102 on June 23, 2008. Miller made his final flight at the age of 101.

You shot me.

Otis Anderson Jr., an American football player on November 29, 2021, responding to his father after the latter fatally shot him.

Everything's going to be all right, old boy.

Terry Wogan, the witty Irish voice. With his charm and banter, he had a choice. From BBC's mic to TV's screen, a broadcasting legend, a satirical dream. Spoke his last words on January 31, 2016, to a priest who visited him.

I'm not afraid. I've done more in my life that I could have ever imagined.

Olivia Newton-John, a musical muse. With her voice and talent, she'd enthuse. From "Grease" to "Physical," a pop sensation, a heartthrob's crush, a global admiration ever before and since dying on August 8, 2022. She was responding to her niece Tottie Goldsmith asking if she was afraid of dying.

Thank God, to-morrow I shall join the glorious company above.

Samuel Drew, the theologian of might. With his pen and parchment, a scholarly sight. From Cornish roots, he rose to fame. A Methodist thinker, with a revered name. With sermons preached and books penned strong, Theology's complexities, he'd prolong. But alas, his days came to an end, A theologian's journey, a heavenly send on March 29, 1833.

Behave Before Being Behaded

I go no further: Approach, veteran soldier, and if you can at least do so much properly, sever this neck.

Marcus Tullius Cicero was a Roman orator and writer. He is considered one of the greatest orators in Roman history and is known for his speeches and writings on politics, philosophy, and rhetoric. He was declared an enemy of the state after the assassination of Julius Caesar and lived up to his reputation as an orator when he spoke his last words to the soldier who beheaded him on 7 December 43 BCE.

Yet I had something there!

André Chénier, French poet, to his friend and fellow poet Jean-Antoine Roucher, prior to their executions by guillotine on July 25, 1794. He did, indeed, have his last famous words.

Pardon me, sir. I did not do it on purpose.

The queen of all apologies? **Marie Antoinette, Queen of France**, apologized to her executioner for stepping on his foot before he chopped her head off on October 16, 1793.

What dost thou fear? Strike, man, strike!

Walter Raleigh, an English explorer, poet and soldier looked at the axe that would be used to behead him, and said: "This is a sharp medicine, but it is a Physician for all diseases and miseries." He followed up his bravery with his final words on October 29, 1618, moments before being beheaded at the Palace of Westminster.

Behold, then, the recompense reserved for the first apostle of liberty.

Camille Desmoulins, a fiery voice, fueled the revolution with passionate choice. His pen and tongue, sharp as a sword, against tyranny, he fiercely roared. But as the tides of revolution turned, Desmoulins' fate was harshly learned. He looked at the axe prior to execution by guillotine on April 5, 1794 and spoke his last words.

My people, I die innocent! (Then, turning towards his executioners, Louis XVI declared) Gentlemen, I am innocent of everything of which I am accused. I hope that my blood may cement the good fortune of the French.

Louis XVI. Even in death, the guy couldn't catch a break. His last words have become the stuff of legend, an iconic phrase that will forever be associated with his tragic downfall. "I die innocent," he supposedly said, as the guillotine blade came down and his head was separated from his body on January 21, 1793. Innocent? He was the king of France, for crying out loud. He may not have personally chopped anyone's head off, but he presided over a system that did. And, not to forget, spending money like it was going out of style, and generally ignoring the needs and wishes of his subjects.

Yes my friend, but it's from the cold.

Stone cold before his death, **Jean Sylvain Bailly**, French astronomer and politician, replied to a heckler who asked if he was trembling as he approached the guillotine on November 12, 1793.

After my head is chopped off, will I still be able to hear, at least for a moment, the sound of my own blood gushing from the stump of my neck? That would be the pleasure to end all pleasures.

Peter Kürten, a German serial killer known as "The Vampire of Düsseldorf" was a sick cunt until his ending on July 2, 1931.

Hold your tongue! Your wretched chatter disgusts me.

Guillaume-Chrétien de Lamoignon de Malesherbes to the priest before his execution. It is unclear if the man with the unspeakable long name got irritated when the priest tried to pronounce it, or if he just was not ready for his last Amen.

Oh Liberty, what crimes are committed in thy name!

Madame Roland, French revolutionary and writer, before execution on November 8, 1793. The French Revolution, that bastion of liberty, equality, and fraternity! What could go wrong when a bunch of passionate revolutionaries take to the streets and start chopping off heads in the name of freedom? As it turns out, quite a lot. In the frenzy of the revolution, some folks got a bit carried away with the whole "liberty" thing and started committing crimes left and right. For example, there was this one time when a group of revolutionary zealots decided to storm a prison and liberate all the inmates. Sounds noble, right? Except that some of those inmates were hardened criminals who promptly went on a looting and pillaging spree, terrorizing the very people the revolution was supposed to be protecting. And let's not forget the infamous "Reign of Terror," during which anyone suspected of being an enemy of the revolution was summarily executed, often without trial or even evidence. Because what's more liberty-loving than killing people for the crime of having a different opinion? Then there was the "Law of Suspects," which allowed the government to arrest anyone suspected of not being sufficiently enthusiastic about the revolution. Because if you're not willing to risk your neck for the cause, clearly you must be an enemy of the people. All in all, the French Revolution was a great reminder that sometimes, in the pursuit of liberty, people can lose sight of the very values they're fighting for. But hey, at least they had some catchy slogans, right?

Long live freedom!

Hans Scholl, co-founder of the White Rose movement. Brother of Sophie Scholl. Words spoke moments before he was beheaded by guillotine on February 22, 1943.

I pray you, gentlemen, in the name of modesty, suffer me to cover my bosom.

Élisabeth of France, sister of Louis XVI, spoke her last words when her scarf fell from her neck before she lost her head and died on May 10, 1794. In the end, Élisabeth's death was a sad reminder that even the most unassuming and unremarkable members of the French aristocracy were not safe from the bloodthirsty mob.

How can we expect righteousness to prevail when there is hardly anyone willing to give himself up individually to a righteous cause... It is such a splendid sunny day, and I have to go. But how many have to die on the battlefield in these days, how many young, promising lives. What does my death matter if by our acts thousands are warned and alerted. Among the student body there will certainly be a revolt.

Sophie Scholl, member of the White Rose anti-Nazi resistance movement. Her final words were before she was killed, on February 22, 1943. Composed of students and a professor from the University of Munich, the White Rose movement produced and distributed leaflets criticizing the Nazi regime, urging Germans to resist, and advocating for a democratic and free Germany.

When I was sixty years of age, I mounted the breach for my king; and now that I am eighty-four I shall not want courage to mount the scaffold for my God.

Philippe de Noailles, Duke of Mouchy, faithful before he was killed on June 27, 1794.

One man have I slain to save a hundred thousand.

Charlotte Corday assassinated Jean-Paul Marat, a key figure in the radical faction of the French Revolution. Corday believed that Marat's influence was responsible for much of the violence and bloodshed during the period, and she hoped that his death would save France from further chaos. Although Corday's actions did not end the Revolution, they may have had some positive effects by paving the way for more moderate voices in the movement. Corday was executed for her crime, but her legacy has been a subject of debate and interpretation after she was killed on July 17, 1793, since beheading was trending for a long time after her death.

I have been unfaithful to God, to my Order, to my King; I die full of faith and repentance.

Armand Louis de Gontaut, a French soldier and politician, was a complex and controversial figure and known for his arrogance and self-interest. He was criticized for his behavior and actions. Some historians have argued that de Gontaut was motivated primarily by a desire for personal glory and recognition, rather than a genuine commitment to the cause of freedom and democracy. It may have contributed to his execution on December 31, 1793.

Better to suffer and to die than to lose one shade of my moral and political character.

Antoine Barnave. A prominent voice in the French Revolution's fray, his words and deeds led the way. But politics can be fickle and cruel, and Barnave met an untimely duel. He spoke his last words before before execution by guillotine on November 29, 1793.

Oh God, have pity on my soul. Oh God, have pity on my soul.

Anne Boleyn, Henry's queen, with beauty that was quite a scene. She caught his eye, led him astray, but marriage vows, she couldn't sway. Accused of treason, a deadly fate, her beheading sealed her tragic state on May 19, 1536.

Mark Smeaton, a courtly lad, who played the lute and made hearts glad. Anne Boleyn's alleged paramour, caught in a scandal's vicious tour. His fate was sealed, his life undone, accused of a crime he never won. Spoke his last words on May 17, 1536, prior to beheading for alleged treason and adultery.

Profanity

Oh, fuck!

Roald Dahl, British author of children's books, before dying on November 23, 1990. After his death, swearing using the word FUCK has been trending, especially popular amongst kids and teens who grew up reading his books. Later those kids discovered that putting those words into human action actually made them moms and dads.

Will somebody please get this fucking cat off my chest!

Filéncio Salmón, a Puerto Rican writer, on his deathbed in 1996. Unclear if it was a black cat. In some cultures, a black cat is considered a symbol of good fortune.

Fuck you.

Tupac "2Pac" Shakur, an American rapper and the voice of a generation. He had a lot to say throughout his career, but his final were simply a good old-fashioned middle finger to the world. They were spoken to the first responder police officer at the scene of his murder on September 13, 1996.

Sorry for saying fuck.

Before he died, **Graham Chapman**, English comedian known from Monthy Python, said sorry to a nurse who stuck a needle in his arm. At Chapmans funeral, his fellow Python, John Cleese held a fucking fabulous speech: Well, I feel that I should say, "Nonsense. Good riddance to him, the freeloading bastard! I hope he fries. "And the reason I think I should say this is, he would never forgive me if I didn't, if I threw away this opportunity to shock you all on his behalf. Anything for him but mindless good taste. I could hear him whispering in my ear last night as I was writing this: "Alright, Cleese, you're very proud of being the first person to ever say 'shit' on television. If this service is really for me, just for starters, I want you to be the first person ever at a British memorial service to say 'fuck'!

Fuck, a bullet wound!

Antonio José de Sucre was a Venezuelan independence leader and President of Peru and Bolivia. He died on 4 June 1830 after being shot in Colombia. He was known for his gentlemanly conduct and had never cursed until that day. Or so they say.

Ugh, Fuck!

Lee Harvey Oswald, the assassin of President John F. Kennedy, after being shot by Jack Ruby on November 24, 1963. Since his death, he has provided job security for conspiracy theorists for decades. He did not do the same for linguists.

Fuck you, motherfucker.

Richard Belzer, an American actor, and edgy comedian spoke his final words on the edge of dying on February 19, 2023.

If you don't like it, you can fuck off!

Keith Moon, an English drummer for the rock band The Who, before he died on September 7, 1978. The words turned out to be his final goodbye to his girlfriend Annette Walter-Lax, after she refused to cook him a meal.

I told u I was hardcore ... u are so fucking stupid.

Brandon Vedas (also known by his nickname ripper on IRC), an American computer enthusiast. He died of a multiple drug overdose on January 12, 2003 while discussing what he was doing via IRC chat and webcam. "I told u I was hardcore" was one of the last things Vedas typed, a phrase often quoted sarcastically on Internet message boards and discussion sites. Vedas subsequently became a strong contender for The Darwin Awards.

You god damned son-of-a-bitch, I am going to kill you!

John Selman, American outlaw and gunfighter on April 6, 1896 before being killed by cowboy George Scarborough.

I have sinned against my brother, the ass.

Francis of Assisi, the saintly chap, preached peace, love, and beggar's scrap. He gave up wealth and noble name, embracing poverty with a holy flame. But when death came to his humble door, even Francis couldn't ignore. He spoke his last words before dying on October 3, 1226.

What are you shooting at?! I'm Pat Tillman! I'm Pat fucking TILLMAN!

Pat Tillman, an American football player and Army Ranger. Last words spoken while he was fatally wounded by friendly fire in Afghanistan on April 22, 2004.

God bless ... God damn.

The whimsical wit, penned tales that were a hilarious hit. His cartoons and stories, a comic treasure, mocking life's quirks without measure. But alas, his humor couldn't fend, death's inevitable, unwelcome trend came knocking on **James Thurbers** door on November 2, 1961.

Kiss my ass.

John Wayne Gacy, an American serial killer and sex offender, spoke his final words on May 10, 1994), prior to execution by lethal injection. Goodbye, Gacy, with your evil ways, may you rot in eternal maze.

You sons of bitches. Give my love to Mother.

Francis Crowley, an American murderer on January 21, 1932 prior to execution by electrocution.

God damn you!

George V, the British King, ruled with a stiff upper lip and a regal bling. His reign saw war, revolution, and strife, but he remained poised with the royal life. When death finally came to his door, the Empire mourned with a solemn roar on January 20, 1936. The Kings last words were to a nurse giving him a sedative. The King was euthanized on the orders of his doctor, Bertrand Dawson, 1st Viscount Dawson of Penn.

I have no need of your Goddamned sympathy – I want to be entertained by some of your grosser reminiscences.

Alexander Woollcott, the literary critic and wit, had a tongue that could surely hit. He dished out sarcasm with a sharp bite, in his reviews, he took no fright. But when it came to his final fate, even Woollcott had to wait before his last breath on January 23, 1943.

I wish to announce the first plank in my campaign for reelection...we're going to have the floors in this goddamned hospital smoothed out!

James **Michael Curley**, the political boss so grand, ruled Boston with an iron hand. Corruption, bribery, his way of life, power and graft, his constant strife. But karma came with an ironic sting, as Curley faced his own reckoning on November 12, 1958. He spoke his last words to his son while being wheeled out of surgery.

You ass-face!

Vicente **Huidobro**, a Chilean poet on January 2, 1948. He spoke his last words after regaining consciousness, he confessed to his loved ones that he was afraid and made his friend Henriette Petit cry, when he stared at her and shouted this expression.

These guys are supposed to be American? My ass!

Boris **Vian**, the Frenchman rare, with wit and words that few could compare. His music, books, and satire so sharp, often left society with a scar. But death came early, a tragic end, cutting short his creative trend on June 23, 1959. He spoke his last words while watching film adaptation of his novel I Spit on Your Graves.

No category

All compounded things are subject to vanish. Strive with earnestness.

Siddhartha Gautama, the Buddha divine, with wisdom and teachings, oh so fine. He left his royal life to seek the truth, enlightenment his ultimate proof. But irony strikes, as his followers grew, wars and divisions, the world never knew. Spoke his last words around 483 BCE.

Heaven has turned against me. No wise ruler arises, and no one in the Empire wishes to make me his teacher. The hour of my death has come.

Confucius, the sage so wise, with teachings that seemed to mesmerize. His ethics, virtues, and profound insight, sought to guide people towards the right. But time and change took their toll, his legacy faced a role reversal toll. Final words spoken around 479 BCE.

For, no Athenian, through my means, ever wore mourning.

Pericles, Athen's statesman so grand, with eloquence that spanned the land. He led Athens to glory and power, but irony struck in his final hour. The plague ravaged, his health did decline, and Athens faced a tragic decline. He was discussing with his friends what his greatest accomplishment had been when he spoke his last words in 429 BCE.

Now, farewell, and remember all my words!

Epicurus, Greek philosopher. "Eat, drink, and be merry!" he proclaimed, a life of hedonism he aimed. But death approached, and irony prevailed, his teachings sometimes derailed. Died in 270 BCE. The majority of his writings are now, ironically, lost.

Weep not, friend, for me, who dies innocent, by the lawless act of wicked men. My condition is much better than theirs.

Agis IV, a Spartan king with zeal, sought to reform with an ideal deal. Land redistribution and equality's might, but faced resistance with all his might. Betrayed by his own, a tragic twist, his noble efforts, failed to persist. He spoke his last words in 241 BCE, prior to execution by strangulation.

This isn't Hamlet, you know, it's not meant to go into the bloody ear.

Laurence Olivier, an English actor and director, to a nurse when she spilled water on him while moistening his lips on July 11, 1989.

Ah! poor hump-back! thy many long years are at last conveying thee to the tomb; thou shalt soon see the palace of Pluto.

Crates of Thebes, a Cynic in town, with a life free of wealth and crown. He eschewed possessions, food and wine, with a lifestyle that seemed divine. But alas, irony struck his fate, for he fell in love with a rich estate. With his last words, Thebes was surveying himself when he was about to die in 285 BCE.

Do not disturb my circles!

Archimedes, a Greek mathematician and star of the Monty Python sketch "Philosophers Football Match" Spoke his final words to a Roman soldier who interrupted his geometric experiments during the capture of Syracuse, whereupon the soldier killed him in 212 BCE.

It is well that we have not been every way unfortunate.

Philopoemen, the "last of the Greeks," a man of war with a temper quite unique. He led the Achaean League with might and skill, but, his luck turned quite ill. He met his end by treachery and deceit, a tragic end for the hero so sweet. In 183 BCE he sent a cup of poison to kill himself after being captured in battle. With his last words he asked the messenger with the poison about his cavalry and was told that most of them had escaped.

Brothers! Brothers, please! This is a house of peace!

Malcolm X, an American activist trying to calm a 400-person chaos with a rhyme, shortly before being killed by gunfire from multiple assailants on February 21, 1965.

Let us ease the Roman people of their continual care, who think it long to await the death of an old man.

Hannibal, a Carthaginian bold and grand, who crossed the Alps with an army so grand. Victories won with elephants and sword, against Rome, a threat they couldn't afford. But in the end, defeat was nigh, as Rome's tactics made him say goodbye in 182 BCE.

It is a cold bath you give me.

Jugurtha, Numidia's prince so shrewd, with cunning schemes he often brewed. Outwitting Rome, he caused them woe, but alas, his luck began to slow. Captured, imprisoned, his fate was sealed, a tragic end to his cunning revealed. In 104 BCE he spoke his last words when being lowered by the Romans into a damp dungeon to starve to death.

O wretched head-band!—not able to help me even in this small thing!

Monime, wife of Mithridates VI, after failing to hang herself by her crown's strings in fulfillment of her death sentence in 72 BCE.

Strike here! Level your rage against the womb which gave birth to such a monster.

Agrippina the Younger, a woman of power and might, with schemes so cunning, she always got her way in sight. She wed her uncle to become a queen, then poisoned her son, so her reign could be seen. But in the end, she was betrayed by her own, a cautionary tale of power overthrown on March 23, 59 CE. She said her last words to her murderer.

Now let the world go as it will; I care for nothing more.

Henry II of England, oh, the troubles that he faced, with sons in rebellion, kingdom misplaced. Thomas Becket, a thorn in his side, a martyrdom that could not hide. Royal woes, and dynastic strife, a tumultuous tale of medieval life. His last words spoken on being told his son John was one of those conspiring against him on July 6, 1189.

Youth, I forgive thee! Take off his chains, give him 100 shillings, and let him go.

Richard I, also known as Richard the Lionheart, was a medieval king who spent most of his life waging war and ignoring his responsibilities back home. He famously abandoned his kingdom to join the Crusades, leaving his younger brother in charge. His death came from a minor arrow wound, proving that even a lionheart can be taken down by a tiny prick. He spoke his final words on April 6, 1199, with reference to the young man who had mortally wounded him with a crossbow.

Ben, make sure you play 'Take My Hand, Precious Lord' in the meeting tonight. Play it real pretty.

Martin Luther King Jr., an American civil rights activist, speaking to musician Ben Branch shortly before being assassinated on April 4, 1968.

Goodnight, my love.

Robin Williams, an American actor and comedian. Last known words spoken to his wife Susan Schneider on August 11, 2014, before he took his own life.

Carry my bones before you on your march, for the rebels will not be able to endure the sight of me, alive or dead.

Edward I, known as the "Hammer of the Scots," spent his reign subjugating Scotland and building castles with wild abandon. His obsession with conquering the Scots was matched only by his love for imposing taxes on his subjects. Death came knocking, but he couldn't tax his way out of it on July 7, 1307. Last words spoken to his son, Edward II of England.

Hold the cross high so I may see it through the flames!

Joan of Arc, the famed warrior maiden, donned armor and led the French to victory against the English in the Hundred Years' War. But alas, her gender-bending ways and divine visions made her the target of religious and political intrigue. In the end, she was burned at the stake, proving that even saints can't escape the fire of human folly. Spoke her last words on May 30, 1431 while she was burning at the stake.

Our Lady of Embrun, my good mistress, help me.

Louis XI, the "Spider King" of France. A man known for his cunning and ruthlessness, but also his love for astrology and his pet monkeys. He married off his daughter to the Duke of Orleans, but only after having her secretly poisoned to ensure she was fertile. His death was probably celebrated by his many enemies on August 30, 1483.

Treason! treason!

Richard III, the "humpbacked" king of England, who famously lost a horse and a kingdom for want of a nail. Known for his ruthless ambition and alleged crimes, he was painted as a villain by the Tudors. His death on the battlefield was a tragic ending to a Shakespearean drama. Or was it? Did he really die, or just go into hiding with Elvis? Last words spoken on August 22, 1485, when deserted by his best troops at the Battle of Bosworth Field.

Let me die to the sound of delicious music.

Honoré Gabriel Riqueti, comte de Mirabeau, was the ultimate political chameleon. He could change his tune faster than a jester in a royal court. One minute he's a reformer, the next he's a counter-revolutionary. He was the master of the flip-flop, a virtuoso of the volte-face. His death came as no surprise, as he had likely changed his mind about breathing on April 2, 1791.

I hope never again to commit a mortal sin, nor even a venial one, if I can help it.

Charles VIII of France, the "Well-Spent," known for his extravagant spending on lavish parties and ill-advised military campaigns. His obsession with Italy led to multiple failed invasions, and his accidental death while hitting his head on a doorframe during a game of tennis is a fitting metaphor for his costly and clumsy reign. Game, set, and match on April 7, 1498.

We heartily desire our executors to consider how behoofful it is to be prayed for.

Henry VII of England, the "Penny Pincher," who hoarded coins tighter than a dragon with its gold. His cunning and thriftiness won him the throne, but his stinginess earned him the nickname "Old Tightfist." Died of natural causes, but surely spent his last moments counting his coins to make sure they were all accounted for on April 21, 1509.

Mine eyes desire thee only. Farewell.

Catherine of Aragon, the Spanish spitfire who outlasted husbands and annulments, giving the term "divorce" a run for its money. Her tenacity and loyalty to Catholicism earned her the title of "Wife #1," until Henry VIII got a roving eye. Died heartbroken, but still the epitome of royal grace and resilience. With her last words she was closing her last letter to her former husband, Henry VIII of England, on January 7, 1536.

After I am dead, you will find Calais written upon my heart.

Mary I of England. Bloody Mary, the fiery redhead with a penchant for persecution. Her religious fervor and zealous crusade against Protestants earned her the nickname "Hot Cross Bun." She briefly torched her way to the throne, only to be snuffed out by illness, leaving England to her half-sister, the "Virgin" Queen Elizabeth. On November 17, 1558. French forces had captured Calais from England earlier that year.

I'm still learning.

Michelangelo, the master of marble, who chiseled and painted his way to immortality. His Sistine Chapel masterpiece left Pope Julius II with a stiff neck and a lighter purse. His famous David statue made sure everyone knew who was the "Big Dave" of Renaissance art. His demise left the art world in mourning, but his legacy lives on in "meme-angelo" jokes. Spoke his last words on February 18, 1564.

They sweat in extremes, for fear of the unwarlike; I am dying undisturbed.

Lucilio Vanini, the controversial freethinker who challenged religious norms with his witty words and daring ideas. His works were hotly debated, his views seen as heresy by some, comedy by others. His fiery personality matched his fiery end, burned at the stake for his satirical views, leaving his critics with a burning question: "Who's laughing now?" Final words spoken on February 9, 1619, prior to execution by strangling and burning for atheism and blasphemy.

It is not my design to drink or to sleep, but my design is to make what haste I can to be gone.

Oliver Cromwell, the Lord Protector of England, a self-proclaimed "man of the people" who rose to power with a revolution and ruled with an iron fist. His puritanical ways and moral high ground were a never-ending source of satire, until his death, when he finally met his match: a satirical epitaph that read, "Here lies Cromwell, who couldn't take a joke.» Spoke his last words shortly before dying on September 3, 1658.

I have seen the glories of the world.

Isaac Barrow, a mathematician so brilliant, he'd calculate the circumference of a donut while waiting in line for coffee. His witty equations and witty comebacks made him the life of the party among academics, until his untimely demise. Rumor has it, he left behind a proof that even death couldn't solve on May 4, 1677.

You are a lier. I am no more a Witch than you are a Wizard, and if you take away my Life, God will give you Blood to drink.

Sarah Good, the original "witch-next-door", with a cauldron full of sass and broomstick wit. She brewed potions that could cure bad moods and hex annoying neighbors. Unfortunately, her spells backfired when she was accused of witchcraft and met an unfortunate end. Turns out, the real witches were just the townsfolk with pitchforks and torches. Last words spoken on July 29, 1692 to Reverend Nicholas Noyes prior to execution by hanging.

I don't know what I may seem to the world. But as to myself I seem to have been only like a boy playing on the seashore and diverting myself now and then in finding a smoother pebble or a prettier shell than the ordinary, whilst the great ocean of truth lay all undiscovered before me.

Newton, the apple guy, and math whiz supreme. He revolutionized physics with a laws galore scheme. Calculus and optics, gravity too, his brain was a force that few could subdue. But, like us all, he met his end, his laws eternal, his legacy to transcend. Spoke his last words before dying in March, 1727.

One hundred and forty-four.

Thomas Fantet de Lagny, a French mathematician, led a fascinating life studying mathematical curves and helping to build the Canal du Midi. However, despite his achievements, his death was overshadowed by the fact that no one really knew how to pronounce his name correctly. Rest in peace, Tom Fanta-de-lag-ny. Last words on April 11, 1734 was responding to the question "What is the square of 12?" on his deathbed.

You are fighting for an earthly crown; I am going to receive a heavenly one.

James Gardiner, a British Army officer. In the heat of the fray, he met his demise, a noble soldier's ultimate prize. He spoke his last words on September 21, 1745, to a Jacobite officer after being mortally wounded at the Battle of Prestonpans.

Don't cry for me, for I go where music is born.

Johann Bach, the maestro of sound, with music that truly did astound. Notes danced and melodies sang, his compositions a symphonic bang! Baroque genius, unmatched in his craft, but, death's final draft. Yet his music lives on, a timeless treasure, his legacy an eternal measure. Left earth on July 28, 1750.

It has all been most interesting.

Mary Wortley Montagu, a witty wordsmith and poetess, was the embodiment of sass and class. Her acerbic pen skewered societal norms, and her biting wit spared none. Her life was a literary dance, and her death a poetic encore. Even in her last breath, she crafted her own elegy, leaving her detractors speechless with her final mic-drop on August 21, 1762.

Dictionary.

Joseph Wright, compiler of The English Dialect Dictionary before dying on February 27, 1930. Advertising it until his last breath.

It is a great consolation to me, in my last hour, that I have never wilfully offended anyone, and that there is not a drop of blood on my hands.

Frederick V of Denmark, a royal misfit, loved lavish feasts and frolics, ruling with an appetite for indulgence. His court was a circus of scandalous affairs, eccentric antics, and exorbitant expenses. But alas, his reign was a fleeting spectacle, and the final act ended with an abrupt curtain call, leaving behind a legacy of extravagance and excess on January 14, 1766.

I could wish this tragic scene were over, but I hope to go through it with becoming dignity.

James Quin, an English actor, spent his life on the stage, pretending to be someone he wasn't. He was quite good at it, but in the end, death played the ultimate role, taking him off the stage for good. He didn't get a standing ovation or a curtain call, but at least he didn't have to memorize any more lines after January 21, 1766.

Throw up the window that I may see once more the magnificent scene of nature.

Rousseau, the philosopher with the "noble savage" notion, lived a life of contradictions. Preaching for natural simplicity, he lived in luxury, fathered children he abandoned, and criticized society while enjoying its comforts. His death was a tragic irony, as he found peace on an island, away from the very society he denounced. Last words before dying on July 2, 1778.

Take me to the boats.

James Cook, the famed explorer, sailed the world in search of new lands to claim for the British Empire. He met many new cultures along the way and even charted the Pacific Ocean. Unfortunately, his voyage ended abruptly when he was killed in Hawaii. Perhaps he should have kept his maps to himself instead of sharing them with the natives! Spoke his last words on February 14, 1779, after being mortally wounded by a native Hawaiian. They probably did not know it was Valentines Day.

The first step towards philosophy is incredulity.

Denis Diderot, the Enlightenment philosopher and writer, was a master of satire. With his razor-sharp wit, he mocked the hypocrisy of the clergy, the ignorance of the aristocracy, and the censorship of his works. He died, leaving behind a legacy of banned books, enlightened ideas, and one epic final punchline on July 31, 1784.

__Cowards! Why did you not defend him?__

Robespierre, the "Incorruptible," led the French Revolution with fiery zeal, preaching equality and justice. But his revolutionary fervor soon turned to tyranny, as he unleashed the guillotine on friend and foe alike. In the end, the revolution ate its own, and Robespierre's reign of terror came to a swift and ironic end beneath the very blade he wielded. Spoke his last words on July 28, 1794, when blamed for the death of Georges Danton.

__I have something to tell you...__

Louis XVII, the "Lost Dauphin," spent his short life in a gilded cage, a pawn in the political machinations of the French Revolution. Despite claims of miraculous escapes and secret survival, his tragic fate was sealed. With no throne to inherit, he met an early demise, a footnote in history's grand drama. Final words before dying in prison at the age of 10 on June 8, 1795.

__I am a queen, but I have not the power to move my arms.__

Louise of Mecklenburg-Strelitz, a queen so fair, Her life and death, a tale so rare. Her joy at her husband's death, a moment of liberation, But alas, it led to her own expiration. In death, she found peace, as Freud would say, But satire, alas, is the only way to portray. Last words spoken before dying on July 19, 1810.

__Contemplate the state in which I am fallen, and learn to die.__

Raphaël Bienvenu Sabatier, a French anatomist and surgeon, teaching his son about his life knowledge as he died on July 19, 1811 .

__I am only sad that I have to leave with a full trunk.__

Béla Bartók, Hungarian composer before dying on September 26, 1945. He died with multiple works left unfinished.

You make me drunk. Pray leave me quiet. I feel it affects my head.

Once upon a time, a princess was born, Destined to wear a royal crown adorned. But alas, her luck took a fateful turn, Her death left the kingdom to mourn and yearn. From a life of privilege to an early grave, A tale of woe that none could save as **Charlotte Augusta** died on November 6, 1817. She was dying of postpartum bleeding.

Although I am a woman and young, I have more than enough courage to suffer this death and a thousand more! Do not forget my example.

Policarpa Salavarrieta, a heroine brave. Fought for independence, her country to save. But in a twist of fate, she was caught and slain. Her death a loss, to Colombia's gain on November 14, 1817.

Bury me where the birds will sing over my grave.

Alexander Wilson, an American ornithologist. His passion for birds, unmatched and true. But, his fate took a tragic cue. A sudden illness, a cruel twist of fate, Cut short his journey, at an early date on August 23, 1813.

Here, here is my end.

Franz Schubert, composer extraordinaire. With music that soared, beyond compare. But life was no symphony, a comedy of errors. From debts to love woes, in various terrors. His melodies touched souls, with their grace. Yet, his own struggles he couldn't efface. A life cut short, a requiem in key, Schubert's legacy, eternal harmony since November 19, 1828.

Walter Pidgeon.

Boris Karloff, an English actor before dying on February 2, 1969. Walter Pigeon is a western Canadian slang term meaning "goodbye". It comes from Pigeon's decision to leave Canada for Hollywood. A fitting remark for someone about to exit this plane of existence.

If I should die, it will not be for the beating I received, but from mortification. I would rather have died than been beaten in that fight.

Simon Byrne, an Irish bare-knuckle boxer. One fight went awry, a fatal blow, A tragic end, a knockout woe. In the ring, he met his untimely fate, A legend gone, from the pugilistic state on June 2, 1833.

I can no longer read or write. De Balzac.

Honoré de Balzac, the writer with a pen so sharp. Creating worlds, with words so dark. From "La Comédie Humaine," a literary feat, with characters flawed, so real and neat. But life was no novel, a comedic play, with debts and woes, day by day. Yet, he wrote on, fueled by caffeine. Till his final chapter, a literary queen. His last words on August 18, 1850 were written across the bottom of a letter from his wife.

Write! Write! Write! Paper! Pencil!

Heinrich Heine, German writer and literary critic. From German romanticism, he'd depart, with satirical quips, a poetic art. But, his health failed, in great despair, in "mattress grave", he'd lay and glare on February 17, 1856.

Mid pleasures and palaces though we may roam / Be it ever so humble, there's no place like home / A charm from the skies seems to hallow us there / Which seek thro' the world, is ne'er met elsewhere / Home! Home! / Sweet, sweet home! / There's no place like home / There's no place like home!

Luigi Lablache, an Italian operatic bass singing his last song on January 17, 1858. After singing the first stanza of Home! Sweet Home! on his deathbed, his voice failed at the start of the second stanza.

Get my Swan costume ready.

Anna Pavlova, a famous cake and a Russian prima ballerina, creator of the role of The Dying Swan, before dying on January 23, 1931.

Tell mother, tell mother, I died for my country…useless…useless…

John Wilkes Booth, the actor, with a violent flair. Assassinated Lincoln, with a gunshot scare. A rebel sympathizer, with a grudge to bear. A deed so heinous, beyond repair. A fugitive on the run, a manhunt wild. Till fate caught up, in a fiery trial on April 26, 1865, after being fatally shot by Boston Corbett.

Please don't let me fall.

Mary Surratt, boarding house hostess. Accused of aiding Lincoln's distress. Hasty trial, controversial fate. Her legacy marred, by justice's debate. Last words spoken on July 7, 1865, prior to execution by hanging after conviction for taking part in the conspiracy to assassinate Abraham Lincoln.

Yes. On the ground.

Charles Dickens, the writer, a literary titan. With tales so rich, they'd truly enlighten. From Oliver Twist to A Christmas Carol, his characters danced, from page to moral. But his own life's twists, a satirical show, from debts to scandals, a dramatic woe. A literary legend, with a troubled past, Dickens' legacy, a satirical contrast. Dickens spoke his final words to his sister-in-law Georgina Hogarth, on June 9, 1870. She had suggested he lie down after he suffered a stroke.

Linen, doctor? You speak of linen? Do you know what linen is? The linen of the peasant, of the worker? Linen is a great thing. I want to make a book of it.

Jules Michelet, the historian, with words so bright. A master of France, in scholarly light. From the French Revolution to medieval days, his histories breathed life, in unique ways. But, his health failed, in great strife, a tragic end, to a scholar's life on February 9, 1874.

Mozart! Mozart!

Gustav Mahler, an Austrian composer and conductor, proving you can never be to famous to be a fan boy on May 18, 1911.

That picture is awful dusty.

Jesse James, the outlaw with swagger so cool. Rode through the Wild West, a charismatic fool. Robbed banks and trains with his gang of merry crooks, making headlines and getting into all kinds of books. Securing a spot in this book with his last words on April 3, 1882, examining a picture on his wall before being murdered by Robert Ford.

We shall go out together.

Marie Bashkirtseff, a painter of fame. Her talent and beauty, all in the name. A feminist, a rebel, with a fiery soul. But her life was cut short, a tragic toll. While looking at a candle beside on her deathbed, she spoke her final words on October 31, 1884.

The sadness will last forever.

Vincent van Gogh, an artist so bright. His colors and swirls, a mesmerizing sight. He painted with passion, with feverish glee. But critics just scoffed, "What's this, Van Gogh? Wee!" He cut off his ear, oh what a scene. Sent it as a gift, just a little obscene. His art sold for peanuts, fame came too late. Now he's a legend, a tortured artist's fate. Last words written in a letter before dying on July 29, 1890.

I feel sick. The dog is sick, too. We are both ill. It must be something we have eaten.

Émile Zola, a writer so bold. Exposed scandals, stories untold. From "J'accuse!" to "Nana" he wrote. But enemies he made, oh what a quote! Accused of libel, a courtroom brawl. Defending truth, standing tall. Though he won the case, it took its toll, Zola's wit and satire, a literary soul. Last words spoken before dying of carbon monoxide poisoning from an improperly ventilated chimney.

To die this way is stupid... And it would please so many scoundrels!... This very night, Magalhães, I could have died for the Republic!

Miguel Bombarda, a Portuguese psychiatrist, after being shot by a mental patient on October 3, 1910.

Well, if it must be so.

Edvard Grieg, a composer so grand. His music from Norway, an enchanted land. From "Peer Gynt" to "In the Hall of the Mountain King", his melodies made the critics sing. Spoke his last words before dying on September 4, 1907.

Give me my glasses.

Mark Twain, a wordsmith so wise. Penning tales that made folks prize. From Huck Finn to Tom Sawyer's fun, he spun yarns that kept readers on the run. With satire sharp and wit so keen, he mocked society, oh so mean. But Twain's own life, a rollercoaster ride, till he breathed his last, with a smirk so wide on April 21, 1910.

Yes, I have heard of it. I am very glad.

Edward VII, a prince of delight. Living life with hedonistic might. A king-to-be, with a penchant for play, from cigars to fashion, in a dapper display. He charmed the ladies, on many a spree. With mistresses galore, oh, what a decree! But the crown he finally wore with pride, till death took him, on a last royal ride on May 6, 1910. His last words spoken after being told by his son that one of his horses had won a race.

No.

Alexander Graham Bell, a Scottish-American inventor, did not call to say I love you when when dying on August 2, 1922. He was replying to his deaf wife Mabel's plea "Don't leave me", signing 'no' in sign language.

These then are my last words to you. Be not afraid of life. Beieve that life is worth living and your belief will help create the fact.

William James, the "Father of American psychology," lived a long and fulfilling life, writing masterworks on the human psyche and founding the psychological movement of functionalism. He died at the ripe old age of 68, leaving behind a legacy that will be remembered for centuries to come. Or at least until the next philosopher comes along and steals his thunder. Last words before dying on August 26, 1910.

I am just going outside and may be some time.

Lawrence Oates, British army officer and Antarctic explorer (17 March 1912), prior to walking out of tent and into blizzard on Terra Nova Expedition.

Last Entry — For God's sake look after our people.

Robert Falcon Scott, Royal Navy officer and Antarctic explorer (29 March 1912). His final diary entry on doomed Terra Nova Expedition.

Go ahead, we will get into one of the other boats.

Carl Oscar Vilhelm Gustafsson Asplund, Swedish-American farmer dying on April 15 , 1912. To his wife, Selma Johansson Asplund, asking her to board a lifeboat with two of their children during the sinking of the Titanic. Carl Asplund and three of his sons perished. His daughter Lillian Asplund was the last living American survivor of the disaster, dying in 2006.

The ladies have to go first.... Get into the lifeboat, to please me.... Good-bye, dearie. I'll see you later.

John Jacob Astor IV, American businessman on April 15, 1912, remaining aboard the RMS Titanic while his pregnant wife boarded a lifeboat.

Well boys, do your best for the women and children, and look out for yourselves.

Edward Smith, sea captain of the RMS Titanic on April 15, 1912, giving orders to crew members before the final plunge of the sinking ship.

Splendid. The finale just a little too fast.

Ysaÿe's fiddle charmed the crowd, But life's symphony wasn't allowed. His final bow, the curtain drew, Leaving a timeless virtuoso cue on May 12, 1931, after his Fourth Sonata was played for him.

Good dog.

Vladimir Lenin, led the Bolshevik crew. Dreamed of revolution anew. His Marxist doctrine, so profound, made the Romanovs kiss the ground. Utopian dreams, oh so grand. But power's grip slipped from his hand. His body now preserved in red, like a tourist trap, he's still not dead. Lenin spoke his final words on January 21, 1924, to his dog who brought him a dead bird.

Don't pull down the blinds. I want the sunlight to greet me.

Rudolph Valentino was a dapper dude. Sultry eyes and tango moves. His sex appeal, oh so rare, made the ladies stop and stare. He starred in films with passion bold. But scandals made his life unfold. His death at thirty, quite a blow, a legend gone, but his hips still glow. Spoke his last words to a nurse on August 23, 1926.

Curtain! Fast music! Lights! Ready for the last finale! Great! The show looks good. The show looks good.

Florenz Ziegfeld Jr. His Follies, a dazzling spree, Showbiz dreams turned tragedy. Curtain closed, the stage grew dark, Leaving a legend's final mark on July 22, 1932.

Freddie Mercury, the British lead vocalist of Queen on November 24, 1991, to his assistant Peter Freestone, before he slipped into a coma and died shortly thereafter.

You heard me, Mike.

John Barrymore's charm, a silver screen delight. But excesses dimmed his starry light. The curtain closed, a tragic end, a legend's legacy, forever penned on May 29 , 1942. Last words spoken to his brother, Lionel Barrymore, who had failed to understand something he said.

Oh God!

Mahatma Gandhi's fight for peace, his guiding light, A loincloth and spinning wheel in sight. But bullets brought a martyr's fall, His legacy, a lasting call since January 30, 1948).

I feel this time they have succeeded. I do not want them to undress me. I want you to undress me.

Leon Trotsky, the revolutionary star. Fought for communism from afar. With fiery speeches and a mighty pen. He riled up comrades now and then. But Stalin's wrath, a deadly foe. Sent an ice pick, dealt the blow. In Mexico, Trotsky met his end. Revolutionary dreams, no longer penned after August 21, 1940 when he spoke his last words to his wife, Natalia Sedova, while being prepared for surgery after being mortally wounded by assassin Ramón Mercader.

Harmony.

Arnold Schoenberg's atonal quest, a musical maze, Traditionalists left in a daze. Legacy avant-garde, a daring swing, Leaving some scratching heads, questioning. Dying in harmony on July 13, 1951.

That guy's gotta stop... He'll see us.

James Dean's rebel charm, a silver screen bliss, But fame's price, a tragic twist. A crash cut his life too soon, leaving a legend, forever in tune. Final words on September 30, 1955 to his friend Rolf Wütherich, moments before the car crash that killed him.

Goodbye, kid. Hurry back.

Hmphrey Bogart's cool, tough-guy allure. From Casablanca to Maltese Falcon's cure. Cigs and fame, a lethal blend, cancer's grip, a tragic end on January 14, 1957. He spoke his last words to his wife Lauren as she left to collect their children.

Say goodbye to Pat, say goodbye to the president and say goodbye to yourself, because you're a nice guy... I'll see... I'll see.

Marilyn Monroe, bombshell blonde with grace. On-screen charm, left hearts in chase. Off-screen life, plagued with strife, mysterious death, a Hollywood knife. Last words spoken over the phone to Peter Lawford, John F. Kennedy's brother-in-law, on August 4, 1962.

Maria.

Nat King Cole, a voice so pure. Racism's grip, an unjust cure. Gone too soon, a legend's fate, his music lives on, forever great since February 15, 1965. Cole was saying his wife's name to a hospital nurse.

I need help bad, man.

Jimi Hendrix, guitar god supreme. Fingers that danced, strings that screamed. Rockstar lifestyle, a double-edged sword, fiery end, music forever adored. Last words spoken to his manager, Chas Chandler, in an answering machine message he left for him on September 18, 1970.

I feel pain here.

Charles de Gaulle, France's leader grand. With stoic frown and commanding hand. Opinions split, a legacy debated, political drama, controversies unabated. De Gaulle was pointing at his neck seconds before he unexpectedly died from aneurysm on November 9, 1970.

Oh, you young people act like old men. You are no fun.

Josephine Baker, iconic dancer and muse. Banana skirt, a bold refuse. Civil rights activist, taking up fights, legacy shines, beacon of light. Last words before she passed away on April 12, 1975.

Mother, I'm going to get my things and get out of this house. Father hates me and I'm never coming back.

Marvin Gaye sang with soul and swayl Family feud cut his life away. Shot by his own father, oh what a tragedy. Silenced a legend, a musical majesty, on April 1, 1984. Gaye spoke his last words moments before being shot to death by his dad.

I'm going to the bathroom to read.

Elvis Presley, King of rock and roll. Fame's wild ride, took its toll. Music's legend, hips that swayed. But excess led, a tragic fade on August 16, 1977.

No paparazzi, I want anonymity.

River Phoenix, an American actor before his very public death on October 31, 1993.

I love you.

Hergé's Tintin, a comic sensation. Thrilling readers with each destination. His artistic flair, a cherished art. But, his final chapter, a heavy heart on March 3, 1983.

I love you very much, my dear Beaver.

Jean-Paul Sartre, the philosopher, deep in thought. Existential musings, theories taught. With pipe and glasses, a brooding air. Intellectual prowess, beyond compare. But love and scandal, a tangled web. With Simone de Beauvoir, an unconventional ebb. Death's curtain fell, life's final act, existentialism's legacy, an intellectual fact. Spoke his final words to his partner, Simone de Beauvoir, on April 15, 1980.

Katie, Katie, look, it'll be fine, you know, I just need to get some sleep.

Heath Ledger, a brilliant actor's name. From "10 Things" to "Brokeback," his fame. But his Joker role, an iconic feat, showed us a villain we couldn't unseat. Sadly, addiction's grip took hold. And his life's tale sadly told on January 22, 2008. Final words on the phone to his sister, before accidentally taking a lethal cocktail of prescription medications.

Money can't buy life.

Bob Marley spread love and cheer. With reggae music that was dear. Cancer took him far too soon, but his legacy still sings a tune. Last words before dying on May 11, 1981.

Just don't leave me alone.

John Belushi, comic delight. Wild and funny day and night. Drugs took hold, an early demise, left us with tears and fond goodbyes on March 5, 1982.

More milk.

Michael Jackson. Pop's reigning king. Moonwalked and sang with flashy bling. Scandals, surgeries, Neverland's zoo. A media circus, but fans stayed true. Sudden death, speculations rife. A tragic end to a legendary life on June 25, 2009. Jackson was asking his doctor for more propofol shortly before he died from an overdose of the same drug.

Don't cry for me. I'm going to be with your father now.

Jackie O, the First Lady queen. With style and grace, always seen. From Camelot to Onassis, she did soar. Lost her loves, but her legend roars. Jackie spoke her final words on May 19, 1994, to her daughter Caroline and son John.

It's time.

Johnny Cash, the "Man in Black" tale. With music that could never fail. Rebel spirit, troubled past, but his legend forever will last. From Folsom Prison to love's embrace, his music burns with timeless grace since September 12, 2003. His last words was responding to his physical therapist after being unable to complete any of his therapy for the day due to his extremely poor health. Later that day he was rushed to the hospital where he died after his health suddenly plummeted.

It's all been rather lovely.

John Le Mesurier, a comedic treasure, Laughs aplenty, beyond measure. With wit and charm, a British delight, his final exit, a sad night on November 15, 1983.

You're a lifesaver, Andy.

William Donaldson, satirical wit. Quirky, bold, a humor hit. From "The Foolish Dictionary" to his name, a satirist, leaving us in acclaim. But his final chapter, a comic end, a legend lost, a satirical friend. Last words spoken to the caretaker of his building, who had collected pills for him on June 22, 2005.

I love you.

Patrick Swayze, a talent rare. Dancing moves and heartthrob flair. Dirty Dancing, Ghost's love tale, but cancer's grasp, a final veil on September 14, 2009. Last words spoken to his wife, Lisa Niemi.

I don't want to die, please don't let me die.

Hugo Chávez, Venezuelan statesman on March 5, 2013. The former president of Venezuela, lived a life of luxury while his country suffered under his rule. He championed socialism and spent lavishly on himself and his cronies, while his people went hungry. His death was mourned by some, but for the majority, it was a welcome end to a disastrous regime. In the end, he left behind a legacy of corruption and mismanagement. whispering unable to speak.

Music has been my doorway of perception and the house that I live in.

David Bowie. The rockstar of space. He knew how to put on a show and ace. From Ziggy Stardust to Thin White Duke, he changed personas more than his leather boots. The man with songs that will forever thrive, who left us mere mortals feeling alive. Said his last words to his friend Gary Oldman on January 10, 2016.

I love you. Take care of the boys.

Larry King, the man in suspenders. Interviewed the elite, the big spenders. His voice was heard across the land, but sadly, he's no longer lending a hand. Last words spoken to his estranged wife, Shawn Southwick, before dying on January 23, 2021.

There is no other life but the eternal.

Phillips Brooks, a man of the cloth. With sermons that could make crowds froth. His words, like fire, stirred the soul, episcopal shepherd, on a spiritual stroll. But when his time came, he met his fate, preaching his way to heaven's gate. This was his final written words before dying on January 23, 1893.

I know I am going where Lucy is.

Rutherford B. Hayes, the 19th president of the United States, was known for his impeccable fashion sense and luxurious facial hair. Some say he won the presidency solely based on his impressive beard. Unfortunately, his presidency was as forgettable as his name, leaving little impact on American history except for his impressive grooming habits. He died on January 17, 1893. His last words referred to his wife, Lucy Webb Hayes, who died in 1889.

I know that it will be well with me.

John Flavel, preacher with fiery might. His sermons lit up hearts each night. From "The Mystery of Providence" to "Husbandry Spiritual," his Puritan wisdom, divinely ritual. But when his time came, his voice did cease, leaving us with a sense of peace. (And Flavel seemed to be strong in his faith as he spoke his last words on June 26, 1691).

So this is what it is like to die – it takes a long time!

Anatole France, a French writer, died on October 12, 1924. Yes, it takes roughly a lifetime before you die.

If this is dying, then I don't think much of it.

Lytton Strachey was an English writer. It is possible he did not need to think much more of it after passing away on January 21, 1932.

So this is death. Well...

Scottish author and philosopher **Thomas Carlyle** philosophized and died on February 5, 1881.

Dying, dying.

Thomas Hood was an English poet and known as a humorist. His last words before he died on May 3, 1845, is still known as boring, boring.

I'm bored... I'm bored.

Gabriele D'Annunzio, an Italian author, on March 1, 1938. He is merely quoted in this book to underline the above point.

Happy.

Raphael, maestro with brush in hand. Painted masterpieces, world-renowned, From "The School of Athens" to "Madonna and Child". His art, divine and undefiled, but life's canvas, sadly torn, a master's legacy, forever worn - and happy when died on April 6, 1520.

I'm bored.

James Baldwin, an American author, on December 1, 1987. Contrary to popular belief, he spoke his last words before the publication of this book.

How beautiful!

Giovan Battista Nani, Venetian ambassador and historian, leaving a glimpse of how it is to die on November 5, 1678.

Happy, happy.

Andrew Combe, a Scottish physician. Well, being a physician is just such a joy. The long hours, the never-ending paperwork, the constant exposure to germs - what's not to love? Dealing with all those pesky patients? There may be no wonder he died happily on August 9, 1847.

I am so happy, so happy.

Gerard Manley Hopkins, poet's delight. With words that soared, and rhymes took flight. From "Pied Beauty" to "The Windhover" bold, his poetry, a treasure to behold. But when his time came, his pen went still, leaving us with a poetic thrill on June 8, 1889.

Who is that?

Prince Albert Victor, Duke of Clarence and Avondale - a man who lived a life of luxury and privilege. He was known for his love of fine dining and excessive partying. Sadly, his wild lifestyle caught up with him and he passed away at the young age of 28, leaving behind a legacy of fancy hats and empty champagne bottles. He repeated his last words over and over again while dying on January 14, 1892.

I see such things as you can not dream of.

William Allingham, wordsmith of the green. Penned verses with an Irish sheen. From "The Fairies" to "The Winding Banks of Erne," his poetry, a lyrical yearn. But when his time came, his pen fell silent, leaving us with verses, truly vibrant, when dying on November 18, 1889.

Woe, I think I'm becoming a god. An emperor should die on his feet!

Vespasian, the Roman emperor, was ironically alluding to the Roman practice of worshipping the dead, before he collapsed on 24 June 79 CE. He then died when attempting to stand up.

I do not suffer, my friends. I only feel a certain difficulty of living.

Bernard Le Bovier de Fontenelle reached the whopping age of 99 and died on January 9, 1757. People at the time must have wondered what he was eating. Not so many may have wondered why he felt some difficulty living when he passed.

O Paradise! O Paradise! At last comes to me the grand consolation. My prisons disappear; the great of earth pass away; all before me is rest.

Silvio Pellico was an Italian writer and poet who lived from 1789 to 1854. His most famous work is "Le mie prigioni" ("My Prisons»). It is not known if he escaped his prison when he died on January 31, 1854.

Now comes the mystery.

Henry Ward Beecher, preacher with might. His sermons packed quite the spiritual bite. From abolition to temperance cause, he fought for justice, applause and applause. But when his time came, he met his fate, leaving behind a pulpit debate on March 8, 1887.

If I had strength to hold a pen, I would write down how easy and pleasant a thing it is to die.

William Hunter, anatomy's sage. Dissecting bodies, page by page. From medical lectures to surgical skill, his knowledge, a scholarly thrill. But when his time came, he breathed his last, anatomical legacy unsurpassed on March 30, 1783.

The taste of death is upon my lips... I feel something, that is not of this earth.

Wolfgang Mozart, a musical prodigy. Composing symphonies with youthful glee. From "Eine kleine Nachtmusik" to "Requiem" grand, his melodies, a masterpiece at hand. But when his time came, he left the stage, a Mozartian legacy, beyond his age. Last words spoken on December 5, 1791.

There is another and a better world.

John Palmer, actor extraordinaire. With talents that made audiences stare. From Shakespearean plays to comedic delight, he charmed the stage with his acting might. But when his time came, the curtains fell, a thespian's farewell, a final spell on August 2, 1798.

This is a beautiful world.

Johann Reinhold Forster, man of divinity and science too. Preached the gospel and studied nature anew. From flora to fauna, his curiosity soared, a pastor-naturalist, divinely floored. But when his time came, he left Earth's sphere, a scholarly legacy, oh so clear. Spoke his final words before dying on December 9, 1798.

No noise, no music, no bohemia!

French author **Henri Murger** suggested being dead is dull on January 28, 1861.

Many things are growing clearer and clearer to me.

Friedrich Schiller, a polymath bright. From writing to philosophy, a mind so light. With plays like "William Tell" and "Don Carlos" grand, his literary prowess, forever will stand. But when his time came, he breathed his last, leaving a legacy, unsurpassed on May 9, 1805.

O, that glorious sun!

Beilby Porteus, a bishop so divine. Fighting for abolition, an unwavering line. From the pulpit to parliament, he raised his voice, against slavery's horrors, he made a choice. But when his time came, he passed away, leaving a legacy, to guide the way since May 13, 1809.

Taking a leap into the dark. O mystery!

Thomas Paine. A revolutionary thinker, born across the sea. Championed freedom and equality with eloquent decree. From philosophy to politics, his mind so keen, a beacon of change, a revolutionary machine. But when his time came, he left this plane, leaving a legacy, that will forever remain since June 8, 1809.

Let me go... The world is bobbing around me.

Sam Bass, the infamous outlaw, was a real wild card. He robbed banks, stagecoaches, and trains with reckless abandon. But his luck finally ran out when he was shot in the back by Texas Rangers at the age of 27. Looks like he should have invested in some bulletproof chaps instead of a fancy hat before dying on July 21, 1878.

What we know is little; what we are ignorant of is immense.

Pierre-Simon Laplace, a genius renowned. His intellect sharp, his knowledge profound. From celestial mechanics to stats so grand, a polymath extraordinaire, across the land. But when he breathed his last, the world did lament, for losing a scholar of unparalleled talent on March 5, 1827.

We perish, we disappear, but the march of time goes on for ever.

Ernest Renan was a French philosopher and writer who loved coffee as much as he loved pondering the meaning of life. He challenged traditional beliefs with his sharp wit and critical thinking, but unfortunately, his caffeine addiction led to his untimely demise. Let this be a lesson to all aspiring philosophers: never underestimate the power of a good night's sleep. He spoke his last words before dying of being overworked on October 2, 1892.

Is there anybody in the room?

John Abernethy, a witty surgeon renowned. His medical practice, a sight to be found. With humor and sarcasm, he'd entertain, patients and peers alike, with his sharp brain. Last words spoken before dying on April 20, 1831.

Nature, how lovely thou art!

Victor Yvart, the agronomist of renown. His expertise in farming, the talk of the town. From soil to seeds, he had it all figured out. But, his life's work, met a tragic drought, a satirical farewell, to a farmer so devout until dying on June 19, 1831.

Gentlemen of the jury, you may retire.

Charles Abbott, a baron of the court. His legal prowess, a formidable fort. Tenterden was his title, so revered. But, his fate was to be feared on November 4, 1832.

I am suffering, sire, the pangs of the damned.

Charles Maurice de Talleyrand-Périgord, a diplomat so sly. With a tongue that could charm or belie. From French Revolution to Napoleon's reign, he played politics with a cunning brain. But his death, a final twist, made some sigh, for he passed away in priestly guise, oh my! Last words spoken on May 17, 1838, to Louis Philippe I, who had asked how he was.

How slow my death agony is.

She was hailed as "the Divine Sarah" and recognized as the first international stage star. **Sarah Beinhardt** was glamorous, mysterious, provocative, and eccentric, and she redefined stage acting in the 19th century before dying on March 26, 1923.

Wonderful! Wonderful this death!

William Etty, a painter so bold. Nudes his muse, stories untold. In scandalous glory he would revel, with colors bright and forms so level. But critics sneered and scorned his art, until death claimed him, a brushwielder's part. Last words spoken when watching the sunset over the River Ouse, Yorkshire, on November 13, 1849.

Don't disturb me. I am too full. O! what a glorious sight.
Does nobody understand?

Irish novelist **James Joyce**. Does not reveal anything in his dying moments on January 13, 1941.

When you come to the hedge that we must all go over, it isn't so bad. You feel
sleepy, you don't care. Just a little dreamy anxiety, which world you're really in,
that's all.

American author **Stephen Crane** cleared it all up on June 5, 1900.

Life After Death

One never knows the ending. One has to die to know exactly what happens after death, although Catholics have their hopes.

Alfred Hitchcock and English filmmaker, possibly opening a new chapter on April 29, 1980.

I can't see a damned thing.

Morgan Earp, American lawman, to his brother Wyatt; the brothers had each promised to describe to the other what he saw at the moment of death. He died without an answer on March 18, 1882. Fortunately, other saw more (arrow down).

It is beautiful.

English poet **Elizabeth Barrett Browning** gave us all hopeful expectations on June 29, 1861.

It is well.

André Gide, a French author, restoring hope before dying on February 19, 1951.

Horrible. Horrible!

American author **MacKinlay Kantor** squashed all expectations on October 11, 1977.

You are wonderful.

No shit, Sherlock! **Arthur Conan Doyle** was a British author who died on July 7, 1930.

It's the most beautiful time in my life, and death.

American author **William Saroyan** before he passed away on May 18, 1981.

Don't ask me how I am! I understand nothing more.

Hans **Christian Andersen**, Danish children's author, was left for words when he died on August 4, 1875.

It's very beautiful over there.

Thomas **Edison** possibly turned on the lights on the other side of life just as he died on October 18, 1931.

This is the fight of day and night. I see black light.

Victor **Hugo,** a French author making people wonder what black light looks like ever since he died on May 22, 1885.

Oh wow. Oh wow. Oh wow.

Steve Jobs, the founder of Apple, looked at his family moments before dying on October 5, 2011.

Peace! Joy!

British poet **Henry Francis Lyte** seemed to enjoy his parting moments on November 20, 1847.

Peace!

American author **Alden Bradford**. Have inspired hippies since October 26, 1843. Well, not really. But he did build a historic house in Boston.

The issue is now clear. It is between light and darkness, and everyone must choose his side.

G. K. Chesterton, an English writer, philosopher, lay theologian and critic. Seeing the light or darkness on June 14, 1936?

Ella, Ella! Everything is utterly different!

Ernst Enno, Estonian bard so bright. His words a lyrical delight. From nature's beauty to folktales grand, his poetry swept across the land. But life's curtain fell, the final act, leaving us bereft, a poetic fact on March 7, 1934. Last words spoken to his wife before his final breath on

Go away. I'm all right.

H. G. Wells, an English author, and futurist. Hopefully saw his future on August 13, 1946.

Now we can cross the Shifting Sands together.

L. **Frank Baum,** American author, before departing to the magic land of Oz on May 5, 1919.

Oh man! Oh man!

Maximilian of Mexico, a royal of lore. Hoped to rule, but fate had more in store. A pawn in Napoleon's grand scheme, a puppet ruler, it would seem. His reign short-lived, a tragic tale, betrayed and shot, his dreams did fail on June 19, 1867.

How easy — how easy — how easy to glide from work here to the work...

John Howard Raymond, the American educator, was known for his innovative teaching methods. He once tried to teach his students about the dangers of procrastination by waiting until the last minute to prepare for his own lecture. Nah, not really. But he was the first President of Polytechnic Institute of New York University. He spoke his last words before dying on August 14, 1878.

This is the happiest day I have ever experienced on earth. I shall soon be where the wicked cease from troubling and the weary are at rest.

Edward Sugden, a legal. Rose to the ranks of the legal biz. Baron St Leonards, a title grand, with legal prowess at his command. But as he passed to the great beyond, legal disputes, they did abscond. For wealth and power, a legacy true, but, disputes, they surely ensue! Last words spoken before dying on January 29, 1875.

This is the happiest moment of my life!

Adolph Fischer was a German-born American labor union activist and anarchist who met a tragic end. He was executed at the age of 33 for his involvement in the Haymarket Riot on November 11, 1887.

Dreadful! Dreadful!

Frederick Holder, the first Speaker of the Australian Parliament, was a man of great distinction. He was elected and re-elected unopposed, which is a testament to his popularity. However, even his popularity could not save him from the cruel hands of fate. He spoke his last words on July 23, 1909, before he suffered a paralytic seizure in the Chamber and was carried out unconscious.

In a few minutes, think that we will see God, that we will be in Heaven.

Duchess Sophie Charlotte in Bavaria was the epitome of aristocratic privilege, with a seemingly endless supply of money and time to pursue her hobbies. She dabbled in the arts, sciences, and education, but let's be real, she probably had a team of servants to do all the hard work. She died young, but at least she got a fancy funeral and a Wikipedia page. Last words spoken on May 4, 1897 before being killed in Bazar de la Charité fire in Paris.

This is it! I'm going. I'm going.

Al Jolson, the man who lived the American Dream. Born in Lithuania, he rose to fame as a blackface comedian and Mammy singer. Spoke his last words on October 23, 1950.

How beautiful it all is.

Frederick Funston, United States Army general and Medal of Honor recipient spoke his final words on February 19,1917. He was listening to an orchestra play "The Blue Danube" waltz in the lobby of The St. Anthony Hotel in San Antonio, Texas. He then collapsed from a heart attack..

My work is done. The pins of the tabernacle are taken out.

Charles Hodge, the brilliant theologian and professor, was a man of many talents. Funny last words was not one of those, but he tried before dying on June 19, 1878.

It is unbelievable.

Mata Hari, the exotic dancer, was a woman of many talents. She was a mistress, a spy, and a femme fatale. She accepted an assignment to spy for France during World War I, but was later accused of being a German spy. Despite her protests of innocence, she was executed by firing squad on October 15, 1917.

I believe everything I have written about immortality.

William Robertson Nicoll, the Scottish Free Church minister, journalist, editor, and man of letters, was a man of many talents. Unknown if immortality was one of them, he passed away on May 4, 1923.

Oh Mother, how beautiful it is!

Maury Henry Biddle Paul, aka "Cholly Knickerbocker", was a society columnist who coined the term "Café Society". He lived a life of luxury, hobnobbing with the elite, and writing about their frivolous exploits. A true inspiration for those who aspire to be famous for doing nothing. He spoke his final words on July 17 , 1942.

I am happy, because I am going to Heaven.

Alexandrina of Balazar, a Portuguese mystic and victim soul, had only eighteen months of schooling before being sent to work on a farm at the age of nine. Her secret to holiness was love for Christ, and her tombstone reads, "Sinners, if the dust of my body can be of help to save you, come close, walk over it, kick it around, and when you have had enough, gather it up and throw it in my face. I will be happy. She spoke her final words on October 13, 1955.

Life is wonderful. I am wonderful.

Mary McLeod Bethune, born in 1875, was one of seventeen children of former slaves. She went on to become an American educator and advisor to U.S. President Franklin D. Roosevelt. Not bad for someone who grew up in the Jim Crow era. She was wonderful! Last words spoken on May 18, 1955.

Death is so boring. So slow. One only waits for it.

Yeah, some actually wait an entire lifetime! **Robert Elsie**, a Canadian-born German Albanologist, last words before dying on October 2, 2017.

I hear it always. I hear the scream. I know he's waiting for me on the other side.

Ramón Mercader, the Soviet agent who killed Leon Trotsky in 1940, dying in Havana on October 18, 1978 of bad consciousness and lung cancer.

Don't worry. It's all right.

Benny Goodman, born in 1909, was an American jazz clarinetist and bandleader known as the "King of Swing." He rose from poverty to become a virtuoso clarinetist and the poster boy for the Swing Era. Goodman's innovations changed the landscape of American music, and he was an international celebrity by the start of World War II. Not too shabby for someone who left school at 14. Last words spoken to his friend Carol Smith, who discovered him pale and slumped on his couch after suffering an apparent heart attack on June 13, 1986.

I shall look forward to a pleasant time.

John Hancock, a founding father of the United States, was known for his flamboyant signature on the Declaration of Independence. He died at the age of 56, leaving behind a legacy of patriotism and a signature that would forever be a pain for schoolchildren to copy. Spoke his final words before dying on October 8, 1793.

What dost thou here, thou cruel beast?

Martin of Tours, third bishop of Tours, was a man of great piety and humility. He was known for his kindness and generosity towards the poor. He died in 397 AD, leaving behind a legacy of compassion and devotion. It is said his last words as he was dying was to the Devil.

Stop. Change that to say, 'I am yet in the land of the dying, but I hope soon to be in the land of the living.

John Owen, English Nonconformist church leader and theologian on August 24, 1683, when his secretary had written "I am still in the land of the living" in a letter in his name.

I will lie down on the couch; I can sleep, and after that I shall be entirely recovered.

Elizabeth Pierrepont, Duchess of Kingston-upon-Hull, lived a life of luxury and scandal. She was married twice, had numerous affairs, and was even accused of bigamy. Upon her death, she was buried in a lavish tomb, a fitting end for a woman who lived life to the fullest until her end on August 26, 1788.

How interesting this all is! It will be a new experience.

Thomas Gold Appleton. Sharp wit, sharper tongue. Lived lavishly, loved laughter. Death came, he left with a joke. Legacy lives on, a satirical treasure. Last words spoken before dying on April 17, 1884.

I am sweeping through the gates, washed in the blood of the Lamb.

Alexander II of Russia, known as the "Tsar Liberator," was assassinated in 1881 by a group of revolutionaries. His reforms, including the emancipation of the serfs, were groundbreaking, but his death proved that even the most progressive rulers couldn't escape the wrath of their people. He spoke his last words in March 1881, as he was bleeding to death after being wounded by nihilist bomb.

Amazing, amazing glory! I am having Paul's understanding.

Charles Reade, a 19th-century English novelist and dramatist, lived a life full of literary achievements. His works, including "The Cloister and the Hearth" and "It Is Never Too Late to Mend," were widely popular. His last words were referring to 2 Corinthians 12:1-4, which he had been discussing with a relative on April 11, 1884.

Life is still full of joy. Thumbs up for joy and adventure.

Maude Adams, a star of the stage. Brought joy to audiences in every age. Her talents shone, her performances bright, from Peter Pan to Shakespeare's light. But alas, her final act came too soon, leaving us all in a mournful swoon. Her talent, now a ghostly trace, a loss to theater's hallowed space July 17, 1953.

Rest In Power

Sir, I wish you to understand the true principles of the government. I wish them carried out. I ask nothing more.

Nothing says "achievement" like delivering a two-hour long inaugural speech in freezing weather, only to die of pneumonia a month later. **William Henry Harrison** became the first to die in office on April 4, 1841. With just 32 days in office, Harrison served the shortest tenure in U.S. Presidential history.

I love you, Sarah. For all eternity, I love you.

James K. Polk, the 11th President of the United States and a true master of... something, I guess. Because nothing says "legacy" like adding a bunch of territory to the United States and then promptly dying of cholera. He died on June 15, 1849, after speaking his last words to his wife, Sarah Childress Polk. She went on to live for another 42 years.

Yes, indeed, we must fly; but not with our feet, but with our hands.

Marcus Junius Brutus, Roman senator and assassin of Julius Caesar, died after defeat at the Battle of Philippi. He then bade his friends farewell before killing himself on 23 October 42 BCE.

There is but one reliance.

Martin Van Buren, the 8th President of the United States, was a master of political strategy. His legacy includes creating the Democratic Party, implementing the "spoils system" of political patronage, and being the first President born a U.S. citizen. But most importantly, he gave us the glorious term "OK" which is still used today to describe lukewarm mediocrity. He died on 24 July 1862 at his home in Kinderhook, New York.

She won't think anything about it.

Abraham Lincoln, the 16th President of the United States, was a true American hero. He proved that with hard work, determination, and a catchy nickname, anyone can rise to greatness. His legacy includes ending slavery, preserving the Union, and inspiring countless Halloween costumes. Plus, he was tall. His last words were assuring his wife, Mary, that their friend Clara would not mind them holding hands. He was fatally shot from behind in the presidential booth of Ford's Theatre shortly after.

When the machinery is broken... I am ready.

Woodrow Wilson, the 28th president of the United States, was known for his eloquent speeches and his idealistic vision for world peace. He also managed to get the 19th amendment passed, giving women the right to vote, which is pretty cool. His last words are a fitting metaphor for anyone who has ever been president. His health declined for several years before his death on February 3, 1924.

I am grateful for your presence.

French President **Marie François Sadi Carnot** was known for his charming smile and dapper appearance. He could talk his way out of any political situation, much like a Frenchman can talk his way out of a traffic ticket. But his presidency was about as successful as a French invasion of Russia, leaving many wondering, "C'est tout?". He died on June 25, 1894, after being stabbed and spoke his last words to a doctor who told him his friends were there.

I have tried so hard to do right.

Grover Cleveland's legacy is a bit like that one time you won a game of checkers against your little cousin. Sure, you technically won, but no one cares, and it doesn't mean anything. He was a forgettable president who managed to serve two non-consecutive terms, leaving most people wondering, "Wait, who was that guy again?". He managed to get the Interstate Commerce Act passed, but that was probably just a lucky break between vetoing everything else. He died of a heart attack on June 24, 1908, and spoke his last words to his wife, Frances.

Please put out that light, James.

Theodore Roosevelt Jr., the 26th president of the United States, was known for his love of nature, his big stick, and his iconic mustache. He was also responsible for creating national parks and preserving wildlife, but we all know the real legacy of Teddy: inspiring the "Teddy bear," the world's most cuddly political mascot. He uttered his last words to family servant James E. Amos before he died in his sleep on January 6, 1919.

That's good. Go on, read some more.

Warren G. Harding, the 29th president of the United States, is remembered for his legacy of scandals and corruption, which is quite an accomplishment considering he only served for two years. His last words could have been a reference to his administration's corruption or just a positive attitude about dying. They were supposedly a response to his wife, Florence Harding. She had been reading aloud a flattering Saturday Evening Post article about him.

Good morning, Robert.

Calvin Coolidge, the 30th president of the United States, is known for his stoic demeanor and love of naps. He famously said, "The business of America is business," which is a great motto if you're a CEO but not so great if you're a human being. His last words were probably the most exciting thing he ever said before dying from a blood clot on January 5, 1933.

Do not cry, Pepito. Show these people that you are brave. It is a rare opportunity for me to die for our country.

José Abad Santos, the fifth Chief Justice of the Philippine Supreme Court, is remembered for his integrity and bravery in the face of the Japanese occupation during World War II. He chose death over dishonor, which is more than can be said for most politicians these days. He was bidding farewell to his son Pepito before his execution on May 1, 1942.

I have a terrific headache.

Franklin D. Roosevelt, the 32nd president of the United States, is remembered for his charismatic leadership during the Great Depression and World War II. He also managed to win four presidential elections, which is quite an accomplishment considering most people can't even win a game of Monopoly. Roosevelt also inspired the "New Deal," which is great if you're a fan of government spending. He suffered an intracerebral hemorrhage a few minutes after speaking his last words on April 12, 1945.

No, you certainly can't.

John F. Kennedy, the 35th president of the United States, is remembered for his good looks, charm, and untimely assassination. His last words were reported as, "No, you certainly can't," which is a strange thing to say before dying, but then again, maybe he was just being sarcastic. After all, he did manage to get Marilyn Monroe's phone number, so he had a sense of humor. Most sources claim his final words were a reply to co-passenger Nellie Connally. She said, "You certainly can't say that the people of Dallas haven't given you a nice welcome, Mr. President." JFK was shot seconds later and died on November 22, 1963.

Go and show yourself to the soldiers, lest they cut you to pieces for being accessory to my death.

Otho, Roman emperor, stabbed himself through the heart 16 April 69 CE. Rather than continue the conflict with Vittelius and cause further bloodshed, Otho chose to end his own life.

Lyndon B. Johnson, the 36th president of the United States, is remembered for his escalation of the Vietnam War and his obsession with his genitalia (Hello, Jumbo! Rumored to be so big that he never sent a dick pick. He would need a drone to capture the image). He also managed to pass some significant civil rights legislation, which is kind of like a serial killer donating to charity. His legacy is complicated, but at least he gave us something to laugh about with his hilarious phone conversations. He uttered his last words on the phone. Johnson had suffered a heart attack and was referring to his Secret Service agent. When agents arrived, he was dead.

These are my last words, and I am certain that my sacrifice will not be in vain. I am certain that, at the very least, it will be a moral lesson that will punish felony, cowardice and treason.

Salvador Allende Gossens, the former president of Chile, is remembered for his socialist policies and his tragic death during the CIA-backed military coup that brought Augusto Pinochet to power. He also had a pretty impressive mustache, which is always a plus. His legacy served as a reminder that sometimes even a democratically elected leader isn't safe from outside interference. He addressed the nation during the coup d´état, before he killed himself moments later, on September 11, 1973. The date marks a black spot in American involvement ever since.

Don't lift me.

Robert F. Kennedy, an American politician speaking to medical attendants who lifted him onto a stretcher several minutes after he was shot and fatally losing consciousness shortly thereafter on June 6, 1968.

Through too much fondness of life, I have lived to endure the sight of my friend taken by the enemy before my face.

Gaius Cassius Longinus, Roman senator and general, one of Julius Caesar's assassins, on 3 October 42 BCE. He believed his comrade Titinius had been captured by Mark Antony's forces at the Battle of Philippi. Cassius then killed himself.

Help.

Richard Nixon, the former president of the United States, is remembered for his legacy of corruption, deceit, and paranoia. He was like a human version of the game "Mafia," always scheming, and ready to throw anyone under the bus to protect himself. His legacy serves as a reminder that even the most powerful men are not above the law, and that karma has a way of catching up to you, especially when you tape-record yourself committing crimes. Nixon suffered a stroke on April 22, 1994, and spoke his last word to a servant in his home.

Asunder flies the man. No single wound the gaping rupture seems. Where trickling crimson flows the tender streams. But from an opening horrible and wide. A thousand vessels pour the bursting tide. At once the winding channel's course was broke. Where wandering life her mazy journey took.

Lucan was Roman poet forced to commit suicide after joining in a conspiracy against Nero. He died 30 April 65 CE, quoting lines from his own epic poem Pharsalia.

I leave you the example of my life, the best and most precious legacy now in my power. Cherish it in your memory, and you will gain at once the applause due to virtue, and the fame of a sincere and generous friendship.

Seneca the Younger was a philosopher of Ancient Rome. He was also a tutor and advisor to the emperor Nero, who came to power in 54 AD. Seneca was ordered to commit suicide by Emperor Nero in 65 AD. Seneca obeyed the order and died by drinking poison.

I am in debt to so many people. I have caused too great a burden to be placed upon them. I can't begin to fathom the countless agonies down the road. The rest of my life would only be a burden for others. I am unable to do anything because of poor health. I can't read, I can't write. Do not be too sad. Isn't life and death all a part of nature? Do not be sorry. Do not feel resentment toward anyone. It is fate. Cremate me. And leave only a small tombstone near home. I've thought on this for a long time.

Roh Moo-hyun, the former president of South Korea, was known for his progressive policies and his commitment to social justice. Unfortunately, his legacy was tarnished by allegations of corruption and scandal. It's like he was trying to bring change to his country, but ended up being changed by it himself. He killed himself on May 23, 2009.

O wretched virtue! thou art a bare name! I mistook thee for a substance; but thou thyself art the slave of fortune.

Decimus Junius Brutus Albinus known conspirator in Julius Caesar's assassination, was captured and killed while fleeing to Macedonia September 43 BCE. Decimus was quoting from Greek tragedian Euripides before dying.

Let no one weep for me, or celebrate my funeral with mourning; for I still live, as I pass to and fro through the mouths of men.

Quintus Ennius was a writer and poet and considered the father of Roman poetry. Before his death in 169 BCE he dictated the lines to be engraved on his memorial. Ironically, only fragments of Ennius's works have survived to the present day.

Go to the rising sun, I am already setting. Think more of death than of me.

Marcus Aurelius was the last of the "Five Good Emperors" of Rome. Also a philosopher and known for his book "Meditations". He spoke his last sentence to his guard before dying of unknown causes on 17 March 180 CE.

Hurry, if anything remains for me to do.

Septimius Severus, Rome's mighty ruler bold. With ambition and power, his story's told. Conquering lands, with armies so grand. Building an empire, by force of command. But, his reign came to an end, leaving Rome in chaos, unable to mend. Last words before dying in York, England on 4 February 211 CE.

I have lost this fight but I leave with honour. I love this country, I love this nation, strive for their wellbeing. I depart without rancour towards you. I wish you, I wish you...

Milada Horáková, Czech politician on June 27, 1950 prior to execution by hanging on fabricated charges of conspiracy and treason.

Equanimity.

Antoninus Pius was the fourth of the Five Good Emperors Roman emperor. He was uttering his last word as he gave the password to the night-watch before dying on7 March 161 CE.

Death twitches my ear. 'Live,' he says. 'I am coming.'

Virgil, the poet of Rome's great fame. Wrote of heroes, gods, and the Trojan's shame. A literary giant of his day, his works, a classic that forever shall stay. But, his death came all too soon, leaving us without his lyrical tune on September 21, 19 BCE.

You must not pity me in this last turn of fate. You should rather be happy in the remembrance of our love, and in the recollection that of all men I was once the most famous and the most powerful, and now, at the end, have fallen not dishonorably, a Roman by a Roman vanquished.

Mark Antony, Rome's famed general. A master of drama, both grand and trivial. Politics and romance led to his fall, a life of conquest, ambition, and all. Last words spoken to Cleopatra before his suicide on August 1, 30 BCE.

And yet Thou hast conquered, O Galilean!

Julian, Roman emperor, after being mortally wounded in battle against the Persians on 26 June 363 CE. He was known for his attempts to revive pagan religion and culture in a Christian-dominated empire. Julians death marked the end of the Constantinian dynasty.

Don't, don't, don't, this will hurt someone.

R. **Budd Dwyer**, American politician on January 22, 1987. He said his last words to the reporters who tried to stop him from shooting himself on live television.

We messed up. We let our guard down. Please tell everybody to be careful. This is real, and if you get diagnosed, get help immediately.

Larry **Dean Dixon**, a senator renowned, COVID-19 struck, spreading all around. Politics and pandemic, an unlikely mix, His health declined, in a cruel and ironic fix on December 4, 2020.

Dear Team, well my time has come. I am eager to rejoin Joan and Eleanor. Before I Go I wanted to let you know how much you mean to me. Never has a public servant had a better group of people working at their side! Together we have accomplished so much and I know you will keep up the good fight. Joe in the White House certainly helps. I always knew it would be okay if I arrived some place and was greeted by one of you! My best to all of you!

Walter **Mondale**, a political force. Fighting for justice, with a steady course. Vice President, senator, a man of renown, his legacy, forever written in history's crown. This was his final message to his staff before he died on April 19, 2021.

I have taken care of everything in life, only not for death—and now I have to die completely unprepared.

Cesare **Borgia**, a man of intrigue. With a cunning mind, and a dangerous league. A politician, soldier, and cardinal too, Machiavellian tactics, his way to pursue. But, his reign was cut short, as fate dealt him a deadly court. Poisoned or stabbed, no one can say, a fitting end for a man who lived by the fray. Final words on March 12, 1507.

It is a bad cause which cannot bear the words of a dying man.

Henry Vane the Younger, a man of liberty. Fighting for justice, with a fiery intensity. A Puritan, a Governor, a Parliamentarian too, his ideals, a beacon for the oppressed and few. But, his time was short and sweet, as the monarchy regained its royal seat. Beheaded for treason, his death a crime, a martyr for democracy, till the end of his time on June 14, 1662.

I am cold.

Louis-Michel le Peletier, marquis de Saint-Fargeau, a nobleman bold and bright. Joined the revolution, with revolutionary might. Voting for Louis' death, in a daring display, but sadly, assassinated, a political price to pay on January 20, 1793.

Pardon for the prisoners, Bonchamps commands it!

Charles de Bonchamps, a general, a man of war. Fighting for the monarchy, with a thunderous roar. Vendéan wars, a bloody conflict of yore, Bonchamps' legacy, a tale of valor and more. But, his time was cruel and brief, as death claimed him, in a tragic relief on October 18, 1793.

Only a soldier's blanket? Make haste and return it to him at once.

Ralph Abercromby, a Scottish soldier and politician spoke his last words on March 28, 1801. Wounded at the Battle of Alexandria, he asked what had been placed under his head and was told it was "Only a soldier's blanket.

Thank God that I have lived to see the day when England is willing to give twenty millions for the abolition of slavery.

Born in the age of Enlightenment, **William Wilberforce** was a crusader against slavery, a beacon of morality. But, abolition took its toll, his health did fail. Yet his legacy stands proud, unlike his waistcoat's button, which did ail. Spoke his last words on July 29, 1833.

Doctor, I wish you to observe how real and beneficial the religion of Christ is to a man about to die. I am, however, much consoled by reflecting that the religion of Christ has, from its first appearance in the world, been attacked in vain by all the wits, philosophers, and wise ones, aided by every power of man, and its triumphs have been complete.

Patrick Henry, a voice of liberty's might. Fighting for independence, with words so bright. A lawyer, an orator, a patriot grand, his speeches, a fiery force, across the land.. Spoke his last words on June 6, 1799.

Doctor, if I could be the man I was when I was 21 years of age, I would be willing to be stripped stark naked on the top of the Alleghany Mountains to run for my life with the hounds of hell at my heels.

Daniel Morgan, an American pioneer, soldier and politician dying on July 6, 1802. Spoke his final words when his physician advised him to settle his affairs.

So little done, so much to do.

Rhodes, the imperial tycoon. built an empire with greed so soon. Diamonds, land, and colonial might, fueled his ambition day and night. But in the end, his deeds were scorned, as history's judgment was finally borne. Farewell, Rhodes, your legacy brought, a reminder of colonialism's fraught. Rhodes was done on March 26, 1902.

I'm convicted unfairly and I die innocent.

Quisling, the infamous traitor, pledged his loyalty to Hitler's favor. A puppet of Nazi tyranny, he helped spread their reign of misery. But justice came, as it always does, and Quisling faced the people's buzz. Rest in infamy, Quisling, forever shamed, by history's verdict, forever maimed. Last words spoken on October 24, 1945, prior to execution by firing squad.

John C. Calhoun, vice president of the United States, and the states' rights champ, advocated slavery with a pompous stamp. Nullification, secession, his doctrines bold, to protect slaveholders, or so he's told. But history frowns on his racist views, as Calhoun's legacy ignominiously ensues. Spoke his last words before dying on March 31, 1850.

William Henry Vanderbilt, the railroad tycoon, amassed wealth like a greedy buffoon. Inherited riches, ruthless acumen, built an empire with avarice's venom. But when he met his maker's call, his fortune meant nothing at all. Final words before dying on December 8, 1885.

John Pierpont Morgan, the Wall Street magnate grand, wielded wealth with an iron hand. Monopolies, mergers, the richest of men, manipulating markets with a cunning yen. But even Morgan couldn't cheat the reaper's toll, for death cares not for a capitalist's role. Last words before dying on March 31, 1913.

Dying During Christmas

Why not? After all, it belongs to him.

Charlie Chaplin, the comedic king. with slapstick antics, he did bring. From silent films to iconic tramp, his talent set the world a-damp. But irony struck, the world turned sour, his passport lost, he lost his power. Exiled from the land he made great, Chaplin's fate, a satirical twist of fate. With his last words on December 25, 1977, he answered a priest who had said, "May the Lord have mercy on your soul».

Now, God be praised, only one hour!

Christian Fürchtegott Gellert, the poet with a delicate pen. Crafted verses that charmed women and men. His morals preached, his rhymes refined, a poet for the cultured and refined. But, his life was not all grand, For his health, it failed to withstand. And with his passing, his words endure, as Gellert, the poet, found his final cure. Last words spoken after being told he had only an hour to live December 13, 1769.

Dying is a very dull, dreary affair. And my advice to you is to have nothing whatever to do with it.

W. Somerset Maugham, an English author should have taken his advice more seriously on December 15, 1965.

Last tag.

Richard B. Mellon, a mogul with wealth so vast, A banker, industrialist, living life so fast. With philanthropy, he gave back to the masses, But some said, "Too little, too late" in snarky passes. His legacy, a tale of money, power, and greed, A capitalist's dream, but with critics who plead. In death, his fortune and empire remain, A tycoon's saga, filled with both praise and disdain. Last words to his brother Andrew Mellon on December 1, 1933. The brothers had been engaged in a game of tag for more than seventy years.

I'm going away tonight.

James Brown, the Godfather of Soul. With his moves and groove, he took control. From "I Feel Good" to "Sex Machine," he rocked the stage. But his offstage antics, a wild rampage. A funky lifestyle, with scandals and fights. A life of excess, and flashing lights. Brown spoke his final words to his manager Charles Bobbit, before dying after falling asleep December 25, 2006.

Hershey bars will be good enough – they'll be fine.

F. Scott Fitzgerald, the writer of fame. With novels that earned him a literary name. Jazz Age excess, parties and wealth. His words a sharp critique, societal stealth. His legacy, tales of the Roaring Twenties told, but a life cut short, stories left untold. Gone too soon, his brilliance shone bright, A literary legend, extinguished in the night. Spoken before dying on December 21, 1940.

It (the Crown of Scotland) came with a lass, and it will go with a lass.

James V of Scotland, a royal king so bold. His reign was filled with tales both brave and untold. Married twice, his wives' fates were quite dire, but his heart belonged to music and the lyre. His kingdom's woes were a constant dread, till early death, by grief, he was misled. Last words spoken on being informed of the birth of his daughter and successor, Mary, Queen of Scots, on December 15, 1542.

Never felt better.

Douglas Fairbanks, American actor and filmmaker. A man of charm and flair, With stunts and swashbuckling to spare. He climbed the heights of fame's great peaks, On screens and stages for weeks and weeks. But life's limelight can fade so fast, And Fairbanks breathed his final gasp. Leaving behind a cinematic legacy, Of daring feats and silver screen synergy. Final words spoken to an attendant who asked how he was on December 12, 1939.

God damn the whole fucking world and everyone in it but you, Carlotta.

W. C. Fields, an American entertainer, before dying on December 25, 1946. Did not give a shit about anyone but his mistress, Carlotta Monti, who he was addressing with his last words.

They tried to get me — I got them first!

Vachel Lindsay, American poet extraordinaire, had a life that was nothing short of a comical affair. With his penchant for dressing in robes and going barefoot, he'd roam from place to place, sometimes playing the lute. His poems, bold and eccentric in style, would raise eyebrows and sometimes even rile. From critiquing imperialism with a satirical tone, to dancing and singing like a poetic cyclone. With admirers aplenty, and critics in tow, Vachel Lindsay's life was a satirical show! He left his final words in his suicide note on December 5, 1931.

Please don't leave me.

Chris Farley, a comic force. With his larger-than-life antics, a humorous tour de force. From "SNL" to "Tommy Boy," he brought the laughs, but his own demons lurked, with dangerous crafts. Last words spoken to a prostitute, leaving a motel where he spent his last night on December 18, 1997.

I no longer see you.

Almeida Garrett, a Portuguese author, addressed his friend Francisco before he passed away on December 9, 1854. They may have never seen each other again.

My Lord, why do you not go on? I am not afraid to die.

Mary II, the queen who kept calm and carried on, despite being wed to a Dutchman named William. She navigated political storms with poise, but her reign was cut short, leaving England in mourning. It seems even royals can't escape the turbulence of marriage and politics, and Mary's legacy remains a mixed bag. She kept calm and carried on, on December 28, 1694, when the clergyman reading the prayers for the sick paused due to being overcome by grief.

For the name of Jesus and the protection of the church I am ready to embrace death.

Thomas Becket, archbishop of Canterbury. A loyal cleric, but life could be scary. A friendship turned sour, a royal dispute, Henry II's wrath, a perilous pursuit. Exile, conflicts, and church-state strife, a martyrdom tale, with a tragic life. Assassinated in his own cathedral, a saintly ending, though quite infernal. Final words to his murderers before being killed on December 29, 1170.

Long Live the Socialist Republic of Romania, independent and free.

Nicolae Ceaucescu, the former communist dictator of Romania, is remembered for his last words before being executed by firing squad: "Long live the Socialist Republic of Romania!" which is like shouting "Long live the Titanic!" after hitting an iceberg. His legacy serves as a reminder that when you treat your people like garbage, they tend to treat you the same way. He and his wife Elena were executed on December 25, 1989.

It grows dark, boys, you may go.

Alexander Adam, a teacher grand. His pedagogical skills, the envy of the land. From Latin to Greek, he taught with might, molding young minds, from dawn till night until his death on December 18, 1809.

If there is a Christian's God, I am not afraid to trust myself in his hands.

Frederick W. Adams, a doctor renowned. Diagnosing ailments, ailments profound. Patients flocking in, prescriptions galore, but malpractice suits, a legal uproar. Med school debts, insurance fights. Billing errors, sleepless nights. In the end, a heart attack, a tragic blow. Irony, the healer needing healing, life's cruel show. Spoken before dying December 17, 1858. The ever-fascinating phenomenon of doctors who believe in God. Who needs years of medical training and a deep understanding of biology and anatomy when you can just pray to a higher power to heal?

Refresh me with a great thought.

Johann Gottfried Herder, the German philosopher, theologian, and leading figure of the Sturm und Drang literary movement, once said, "A poet is the creator of the nation around him." Unfortunately, Herder's own nation didn't seem to appreciate his poetic abilities, as he died in relative obscurity on December 18, 1803.

May an avenger arise from my bones.

Filippo Strozzi the Younger, the Florentine banker, lived a life of wealth and splendor, but his dealings were not always tender. In a political game, he was caught in a bind, and his rivals unkind. His assets seized, his power diminished, his fate grimly finished. A satirical tale of ambition and greed, a cautionary lesson, indeed. Final words in his suicide letter December 18, 1538.

To Harald, may God forgive you and forgive me too but I prefer to take my life away and our baby's before I bring him with shame or killing him, Lupe.

Lupe Vélez, Mexican actress, dancer and singer. A star so bright. In films, she danced and sang with might. Her fame rose high, her talent clear, But in love, she faced turmoil and fear. A tumultuous romance, a bitter end, Led to heartbreak, she couldn't mend. In a final act of tragic strife, She bid adieu to this mortal life. A tale of glamour, stardom, and fame. With a heartache that no one could tame. Her last words written in her suicide note on December 14, 1944, addressed to actor Harald Ramond. Vélez was pregnant with Ramond's child at the time.

Ron Miller \ Way Down Cellar \ Kirt Russell \ CIA - Mobley

Walt Disney's dreams, a kingdom built, With Mickey Mouse's ears well-tilt. From "Snow White" to "The Lion King", he enchanted kids with everything. But some claim plagiarism, others say, his legacy, a corporate sway. A visionary, a creative spark, his empire grows, even in the dark. His last words were written on the bottom of a page on December 15, 1966. Actor Kurt Russels name misspelled as Kirt.

Too late.

Fernando Álvarez, Duke of Alba, a fearsome name. A Spanish general of military fame. Conquered lands and crushed rebellion with might, but faced unrest and rebellion in his own right. In death, his legacy debated and debated, a polarizing figure, loved and hated. On learning that the King was to visit him, he said his final words on December 11, 1582.

Jesus! I pardon you.

Vittoria Accoramboni, Italian belle. Her life a tale of love and betrayal. Her beauty stirred hearts and caused a stir, but court intrigue would prove a fatal blur. Her death, a mystery, a tale of woe. Who had the motive? We may never know! Last known words before dying on December 22, 1585.

I don't want the doctor's death. I want to have my own freedom.

Rainer Maria Rilke, a Bohemian-Austrian poet and novelist on December 29, 1926.

If you will send for a doctor I will see him now.

Emily Brontë, a literary star. Whose novels near and far. Wuthering Heights, a haunting tale, of love, revenge, and windswept gale. Her legacy, a timeless art, but fame came posthumous, in part. Her death, a loss to literature's lore, yet her works endure forevermore. Brontë spoke her final words to her sister Charlotte, on December 19, 1848.

What an idle piece of ceremony this buttoning and unbuttoning is to me, now.

Richard Brocklesby, the great physician! He cured people, but not without a steep bill. Patients would die of a heart attack after hearing the price. He was so good at his job that he even cured himself of humility. But in the end, even the best doctor can't cure death. It seems he forgot to write himself a prescription. Last words spoken on December 11, 1797, as his servants dressed him for bed.

Shakespeare, I come.

Theodore Dreiser, a novelist of might. Captured the human condition, dark and light. Realism his tool, social issues he addressed, injustice, corruption, and the human quest. His legacy, stories that still resonate, a literary giant, left us to contemplate. Death may have silenced him, but his words endure, a satirical observer, sharp and pure. Ready to meet his idol on December 28, 1945.

My bedfellows are cramp and cough – we three all in one bed!

Charles Lamb, a literary maverick, witty and grand. His essays and letters, a delightful wonderland. With humor and pathos, he penned his way, sharing tales of life's joys and sorrows each day until his death on December 27, 1834.

Maurice Ravel, with music so refined. Melodies and harmonies so intricately twined. From "Bolero" to "Pavane," his works so grand, a legacy of genius, known throughout the land. But, his death, a tragic fate. His brilliance silenced, a symphony cut short, oh so late. Ravel was referring to the bandages on his head after brain surgery with his last words on December 28, 1937.

Samuel Hopkins, abolitionist grand. With sermons fiery, he took a stand. Against slavery's evil, a moral fight, preached equality, with all his might. His legacy, a voice for the oppressed, a beacon of hope, in a world distressed, Though gone from earth, his ideals remain, Samuel Hopkins, a legacy, without stain. Left the world poetically on December 20, 1803.

Saddam Hussein, the former dictator of Iraq, recited the Islamic creed, the Shahada, as his last words before being executed. It was like he suddenly remembered that he was Muslim and thought reciting the Shahada would somehow absolve him of all the crimes he committed. His legacy serves as a reminder that religion can be used as a tool for manipulation and that no amount of piety can make up for the harm caused by a life of tyranny and oppression. He died as he said "and Muhammad" in his second recitation on December 30, 2006.

Alban Berg, the atonal trailblazer, composed melodies that defied convention and made critics squirm. His music was avant-garde, his legacy profound, but the masses scratched their heads in confusion. His final note faded, leaving the world puzzled but applauding. He spoke his last words to his wife December 24, 1935. She had asked him to relax.

Congestion. Stopped.

Joseph Henry Green, the surgeon with a steady hand. In the operating room he'd command. With scalpel sharp and skillful touch, he'd cure the sick, with nary a clutch. His legacy, renowned and wide, as patients praised his skill with pride. Yet, Death's cold grip, he could not evade, for mortal flesh, no cure was made. Final words on December 13, 1863. Green was breathing with difficulty on his deathbed and then taking his own pulse.

I am not able to explain myself.

Bastiat, the witty economist. With satire sharp and logic brisk. Fought against tariffs and protection, exposing fallacies without detection, But, his work was often dismissed. Economic truths, so sorely missed, Till his untimely death, a bitter blow, his legacy lives on, in free trade we now know. Spoke his final words before dying on December 24, 1850.

I see earth receding; Heaven is opening; God is calling me.

Dwight L. Moody, the great evangelist, lived a life of piety and devotion. He preached to thousands, but, even his faith could not save him from the clutches of death. As he lay dying, his daughter cried out, "Father, we can't spare you." But death, as always, had the final say, and took him away on December 22, 1899.

Yet I was once your Emperor.

Vitellius, Roman emperor. Vitellius' reign was short-lived, as his incompetence and unpopularity led to a rebellion. Vespasian was declared emperor by his troops, and he marched on Rome to overthrow Vitellius. In December 69 CE, Vespasian's forces defeated Vitellius' troops. Vitellius was captured, tortured, and killed by Vespasian's supporters. His last words were uttered where he died, on the Gemonian stairs 22 December 69 CE.

Open the gates! Open the gates!

Sarah Wesley, a wife so meek. Endured Charles' preaching, week after week. She supported his ministry with unwavering grace, as Charles wrote hymns at a furious pace. But when her time came, she passed away, Leaving behind a hymn-singing legacy, they say. Spoke her last words moments before dying on December 28, 1822.

How do I get out of this labyrinth!

Simón Bolívar, the "Liberator" of the land. With grand visions and a revolutionary plan. Freed Latin America from colonial chain, a hero to many, his legacy will remain. But when he passed away, his dreams still unfinished, a satirical quip, for a world left diminished on December 17, 1830.

I live.

Aleksis Kivi, Finland's prose wiz. Penning tales that made hearts fizz. From "Seven Brothers" to "Nummisuutarit" grand, his literary prowess spanned the land. But when life's inkwell ran dry and spent, his stories lived on, a timeless vent since his death on December 31, 1872.

Van Halen!

Dimebag Darrell, metal's axe-master. With riffs that shredded faster and faster. Tragically slain by a fan's deranged act, metal world mourned, a brutal impact on December 8, 2004.

Tired—very tired—a long journey—to take.

Kaspar Hauser, a mystery profound. A foundling in town, bewildered and unsound. His origin unknown, his past a riddle, a tale of intrigue that made many a fiddle. But his death, a finale that left us all dumbfound on December 17,1833.

I shall retire early; I am very tired.

Thomas Babington Macaulay, the master of verbosity, whose words flowed with pompous verbosity. His speeches, essays, tomes galore, a treasure trove of verbosity galore! Yet in his grave, he rests in peace, spared from endless verbosity, at least, deceased since December 28 1859.

I miss her so much, I want to be with Carrie.

Debbie Reynolds. From "Singin' in the Rain" to "Tammy and the Bachelor," Her talent and charm were hard to match her. The world was struck with grief when she passed away, But her movies and music will forever stay. Spoken before dying on December 28 , 2016, of intracerebral hemorrhage. She died one day after the death of her daughter, Carrie Fisher.

I'm shot! I'm shot!

John Lennon, rock 'n' roll's peace preacher. Fame, fortune, and an iconic feature. With Yoko Ono, love so strong, Imagine world peace, his lifelong song. But a senseless act, a tragic shot, Silenced his voice, a cruel plot on December 8, 1980.

I love everybody. If ever I had an enemy, I should hope to meet and welcome that enemy in heaven.

Christina Rossetti, a poet quite elite. Her works on love and death, so bittersweet. From Goblin Market to When I Am Dead, her words will stay with us, it's been said. Spoke her last words on December 29 , 1894.

Goodbye, my friend, goodbye. My dear, you are in my heart. Predestined separation promises a future meeting.

Sergei Yesenin, a poet of great fame. Whose words were known to ignite a flame. With verses of love and life so true, but his addiction to booze, oh what a view. The partying and brawls, they took a toll, and left him feeling alone, empty and cold. Last words written in his final poem before allegedly taking his own life on December 28, 1925.

On A Final Note

Football Season Is Over. No More Games. No More Bombs. No More Walking. No More Fun. No More Swimming. 67. That is 17 years past 50. 17 more than I needed or wanted. Boring. I am always bitchy. No Fun – for anybody. 67. You are getting Greedy. Act your old age. Relax – This won't hurt.

Hunter S. Thompson, American journalist and author (20 February 2005). His suicide note was written four days before his death.

Here thou art, then!

Cleopatra, pharaoh of Egypt. Cleopatra, the queen with a cunning plan, faced capture by Rome's man. With venomous wit, she chose a snake's kiss, a dramatic exit, a satirical twist. A pharaoh's demise, in legend she'd be remembered, a queen who died, by an asp's venom rendered on August 30, BCE.

All fled, all done So lift me on the pyre. The feast is over And the lamps expire.

Robert E. Howard, a writer grand. Created worlds with sword in hand. Barbarians fierce, adventures bold, but, his story soon was told. A life cut short, a tragic end, a brilliant mind, a literary trend. Gone too soon, his works remain, a legacy of fantasy, an eternal reign. He quoted from "The House of Cæsar" by Viola Garvin in his suicide note on June 11, 1936.

I haven't felt the excitement of listening to, as well as creating music, along with really writing something for too many years now. I feel guilty beyond words about these things, for example when we're backstage and the lights go out and the manic roar of the crowd begins. It doesn't affect me in the way which it did for Freddie Mercury, whoseemed to love and relish the love and admiration from the crowd, which is something I totally admire and envy.

The fact is, I can't fool you, any of you. It simply isn't fair to you, or to me. The worst crime can think of would be to pull people off by faking it, pretending as if I'm having one 100% fun. Sometimes I feel as though I should have a punch-in time clock before I walk out on-stage. I've tried everything within my power to appreciate it, and I do, God believe me, I do, but it's not enough. I appreciate the fact that I, and we, have affected, and entertained a lot of people. I must be one of the narcisists who only appreciate things when they're alone. I'm too sensitive, I need to be slightly numb in order to regain the enthusiasm.But, what's sad is our child. On our last three tours, I've had a much betterappreciation of all the people I've known personally, and as fans of our music.

But I still can't get out the frustration, the guilt, and the sympathy I have for everybody. There is good in all of us, and I simply love people too much. So much that it makes me feel too fucking sad. The sad little sensitive unappreciative pisces Jesus man! why don't you just enjoy it? I dont know! I have a of a wide who sweats ambition and empathy, and a daughter who reminds me to much of what I use to be. full of love and joy, every person she meets because everyone is good and will do her no harm.

And that terrifies me to the point to where I can barely function. I can't stand the thought of Frances becoming the miserable self destructive, deathrocker she become. I have it good, very good, and I'm grateful, but since the age of seven, I've become hateful towards all humans in general. Only because it seems so easy for people to get along and have empathy.

Empathy only because I love and feel for people too much I guess. Thank you from the pit of my burning nauseas stomach for your letters and concern during the last years.

I'm too much of a neurotic moody person and I don't have the passion anymore, so remember, it's better to burn out, than to fade away. Peace, love, empathy, Kurt Cobain. Frances and Courtney, I'll be at your altar. Please keep going Courtney for Frances for her life which will be so much happier without me. I LOVE YOU. I LOVE YOU!

Kurt Cobain, American musician (5 April 1994), closing his suicide note. Cobain addressed the note to his childhood imaginary friend Boddah.

I am going to put myself to sleep now for a bit longer than usual. Call it Eternity.

The Polish-American novelist, spun tales so surreal, it left readers perplexed and in awe. But as his fame grew, so did the scandal and flaw. His life a satirical whirlwind, with lies and deceit, a controversial feat. In the end, the truth was revealed, and his legacy, forever sealed in his **Jerzy Kosinskys** suicide note ion May 3, 1991.

What Cato did, and Addison approved, cannot be wrong.

Eustace Budgell, the English writer and politico, had ambition and charm, but a knack for ego. With pamphlets and satire, he made his mark, until a political scandal left him in the dark. His once bright career, now tarnished and dire, a cautionary tale of satire's friendly fire. His suicide note, written before drowning himself in the Thames May 4, 1737.

I can yet find words to thank you, sir; it is the most welcome news you could give me. What should I wish to live for?

Wolfe Tone, the Irish revolutionary bold, his zeal for independence, never controlled. He sought to free Ireland from England's grasp, with passion and fervor, an arduous task. But his rebellion thwarted, he faced defeat, a satirical twist, bitter and bittersweet. Imprisoned, he met a tragic end, a martyr's fate, a nation's friend. Tone died in prison November 19, 1798, under unclear circumstances (possibly suicide) while awaiting execution by hanging.

And now with my latest writing and utterance, and with what will be near my latest breath, I here repeat and would willingly proclaim my unmitigated hatred to yankee rule – to all political, social and business connections with Yankees, and the perfidious, malignant and vile Yankee race.

Edmund Ruffin, the Virginia planter, owned slaves and land, a life of grandeur. His views extreme, his racism clear, with delusions of grandeur, he held them dear. But as Civil War loomed, his cause lost steam, he chose to end it all, a satirical extreme. With a gunshot, he passed away, a tragic tale, a slave owner's dismay. Final words the conclusion of final diary entry before suicide on June 18, 1865.

Leandro N. Alem, the Argentine politico, led a life of passion, always on the go. Fighting for democracy, he had a plan, but political rivals, a cunning clan. With a controversial death, a satirical blow, his legacy lives on, a political show. A martyr's tale, a politician's plight, in Argentina's history, a dramatic light. In his suicide note on July 1, 1896, quoting the motto of the Radical Civic Union.

I am sorry that we cause you yet more effort beyond death, and I am convinced that you are doing what you can do (which perhaps is not very much). Forgive us our desertion! We wish you and all our friends to experience better times. Your truly devoted Felix Hausdorff.

Felix Hausdorff, German math maestro, made sets and spaces his intellectual manifesto. He proved theorems with fervent delight, But his Jewish heritage brought a fearful plight.

The position has become impossible.
Anxious important work to do and three commissions of enquiry to attend to. We may not have done as well as possible in the past but we will necessarily be hampered to do well in the imminent future.
I feel that my brain is suffering and I am in great fear of what effect all this worry will have upon me. I have lost control of my thoughts. The Coolgardie scheme is all right and I could finish it if I got a chance and protection from misrepresentation but there's no hope for that now and its better that it should be given to some entirely new man to do who will be untrammelled by prior responsibility. Put the wing walls to Helena Weir at once.

C. Y. O'Connor, the engineer extraordinaire, with vision and skill, beyond compare. He built the pipeline, a water lifeline, for a parched Western Australia, so fine. But critics sneered, and foes conspired, his project mired. In despair, he met his end, a tragedy, unbeknownst to friend and enemy. His legacy lives on, a bitter irony, a hero remembered for his engineering symphony. Purported suicide note on March 10, 1902.

Human life consists in mutual service. No grief, pain, misfortune, or "broken heart," is excuse for cutting off one's life while any power of service remains. But when all usefulness is over, when one is assured of an unavoidable and imminent death, it is the simplest of human rights to choose a quick and easy death in place of a slow and horrible one. I have preferred chloroform over cancer.

Charlotte Perkins Gilman, American humanist and writer. She penned feminist prose, Breaking gender norms with bold disclose. Her tales of women's plight and pain, Made some uncomfortable, others disdain. Her words stirred up a fiery storm, Challenging societal norm. But, her fame brought strife, As critics dismissed her work with a knife. Her story ended with a twist, Her death came as an ironic tryst. No one knew the pain she hid, Her writing silenced, her legacy bid. Charlotte wrote her final words in her suicide note on August 17, 1935.

They demand from me to kill the children of my nation with my own hands. There is nothing left for me but to die.

Adam Czerniaków, an engineer so bright. Also served as a senator with all his might. But WWII brought a tumultuous tide, as he faced the Nazis with courage and tried. As head of Warsaw's Jewish Council, he fought, but impossible choices, he was distraught. In '42, overwhelmed by despair, he took his own life, a heavy burden to bear. A tragic tale of war's brutal toll, he was writing to his wife prior to his suicide. The SS had ordered the Judenrat and the Jewish Ghetto Police to begin supplying 6000 people per day, including children, for deportation. He died on July 23, 1942.

Frenzy hath seized thy dearest son, / Who from thy shores in glory came / The first in valor and in fame; / Thy deeds that he hath done / Seem hostile all to hostile eyes.... / Better to die, and sleep / The never waking sleep, than linger on, / And dare to live, when the soul's life is gone.

James Forrestal, United States Secretary of Defense. A man of might, held power and defense in his sight. But politics, a treacherous game, led to scandals, tarnished his name. A mind troubled, a soul distressed, his mental health put to the test. In the end, a tragic fall from grace, a controversial death took its place. Written in his suicide note on May 22, 1949. The words were a quotation from the play Ajax by Sophocles.

Do not grieve for me. My nerves are all shot and for the last year I have been in agony day and night—except when I sleep with sleeping pills—and any peace I have by day is when I am drugged by pills. I have had a wonderful life but it is over and my nerves get worse and I am afraid they will have to take me away. So please forgive me, all those I love and may God forgive me too, but I cannot bear the agony and it [is] best for everyone this way. The future is just old age and illness and pain. Goodbye and thank you for all your love. I must have peace and this is the only way. Jimmy

James Whale, English film and theater director and actor. the master of horror and delight, Created monsters that gave us a fright. But life's shadows cast a different hue, As troubles haunted him, it's true. A tortured soul, a genius mind, Yet struggles left him feeling confined. His final scene, a mystery unsolved, A tragic end, the world was involved. Final words written in his suicide note on May 29, 1957.

I have laid my papers on a bed for my daughters. I have left the door open for the police to enter. I am going to shoot myself.

Donald E. Montgomery, American economist. With graphs and charts, Montgomery was grand, Economics was his promised land. But theories failed, predictions awry, his models mocked, and budgets gone awry. His tenure short, his fame was fleeting, his colleagues left, the market's beating. A tragic end, in debt he sank, economic woes, a cruel prank. Last words spoken on October, 11 1957), when calling police before committing suicide.

Dear Hef, When you read this I shall be dead. I cannot go on living with myself and hurting those dear to me. What I do has nothing to do with you.

Jack Cole, American cartoonist. Cole, the comic maven, Drew Plastic Man with wit engraven. Stretchy hero, so absurd. Saved the day, but never heard. Laughter his weapon, ink his tool. With zany antics, he'd just fool. But fame and fortune, fleeting friends. Life's struggles, unforeseen bends. A tragic twist, a sudden fall. The cartoonist's final call. Gone too soon, his art remains, a satirical legacy that still entertains. Final words in his suicide note to Hugh Hefner before dying on August 13, 1958.

Blame only the regime for my death.

Romas Kalanta, Lithuanian high school student. Young Romas Kalanta, full of zeal, Protested Soviet rule, with fiery appeal. A daring act, a stand so bold, His story of defiance soon was told. But alas, his fate was grim and dire, Oppression's wrath set his world on fire. In flames he perished, a martyr's end, His legacy lives on, a freedom's trend. Last words prior to committing suicide by self-immolation to protest the Soviet regime in Lithuania on May 14, 1972.

In keeping with the WXLT practice of presenting the most immediate and complete reports of local blood and guts news, TV 40 presents what is believed to be a television first. In living color, exclusive coverage of an attempted suicide.

Christine Chubbuck, American news anchor for WWSB (formerly known as WXLT). a news anchor bold. Her on-air antics, a story to be told. With serious news, she did compete, she scripted her own demise, quite a feat. On live TV, a tragic twist, as she pulled the trigger, her point was missed. Words spoken immediately before shooting herself in the head on air July 15, 1974.

I must end it. There's no hope left. I'll be at peace. No one had anything to do with this. My decision totally. Freddie Prinze. P.S. I'm sorry. Forgive me. Dusty's here. He's innocent. He cared.

Freddie Prinze, American actor/comedian. a funny man so bright, Brought laughter with his comedic might. But fame and fortune took their toll, As he battled demons that took their toll. In a moment of despair and strife, He tragically ended his own life. A satire of fame's dark side, A cautionary tale, a comedic ride. Final words written in his suicide note. He shot himself in the head in front of his business manager , while under the influence of prescription drugs on January 29, 1977.'Dusty' refers to Marvin Snyder, Prinze's business manager who attempted to stop Prinze from taking his own life.

Dalida, Italian-French singer and actress a songbird on the stage. Her beauty and talent all the rage. But beneath the glitz and glamour show, lay the pressure that began to grow. Her life a whirlwind of fame and clout, yet sadness lurking, without a doubt. Her voice soared high, but her heart felt low, as she struggled with demons few could know. In the end, she couldn't bear the strain, a tragic loss, a heart filled with pain. A satire of stardom's dark demands, a cautionary tale in far-off lands. From her suicide note on May 3, 1987.

I'm really, really sorry. The pain of life overrides the joy to the point that joy does not exist... depressed... without phone... money for rent... money for child support... money for debts... money!!!... I am haunted by the vivid memories of killings & corpses & anger & pain... of starving or wounded children, of trigger-happy madmen, often police, of killer executioners... I have gone to join Ken if I am that lucky.

Kevin Carter, South African photojournalist. The famed lensman, captured the world's strife with his camera. Critics hailed his Pulitzer-winning shots, but decried him as a "vulture" for exploiting suffering. Battling inner demons, he met a tragic end. Satirical irony, a cautionary tale of fame's cost and war's toll, left us pondering: Who captured whom? Words in his suicide note on July 27, 1994. Carter took one of the most iconic photographs of the century – a Sudanese child, starved almost to death, crouching with her head buried in her tiny hands while a vulture awaits her death so that it could devour the corpse.

This is for you!

Ricardo López, Uruguayan-born American pest controller. Pest control whiz, with sprays and traps, he'd sure show his biz! But fame was fleeting, a quirky fate, he snapped, sent a bomb to his idol's gate. A satirical twist, bizarre and wild, his life cut short, pest control gone wild! Last words on September 12, 1996 before committing suicide with a gun after he mailed a bomb to Icelandic musician Björk, attempting to kill her.

The act of taking my own life is not something I am doing without a lot of thought. I don't believe that people should take their own lives without deep and thoughtful reflection over a considerable period of time. I do believe strongly, however, that the right to do so is one of the most fundamental rights that anyone in a free society should have. For me much of the world makes no sense, but my feelings about what I am doing ring loud and clear to an inner ear and a place where there is no self, only calm. Love always, Wendy.

Wendy O. Williams, American singer, songwriter and actress. Punk rock queen, fierce and bold, on the scene. Plastered with paint, chains and spikes, she belted out with raucous likes. Her life a whirlwind, wild and free, but fame's price high, it seems to be. In the end, a tragic fate, her voice silenced, punk rock's late on April 6, 1998.

Carol, I am so sorry for this. I feel I just can't go on. I have always tried to do the right thing but where there was once great pride now it's gone. I love you and the children so much. I just can't be any good to you or myself. The pain is overwhelming. Please try to forgive me. Cliff—J. Clifford Baxter.

J. Clifford Baxter, Enron executive. Enron's man on the rise, soaring high, counting profits in the skies. With schemes and deals, he played his part, but Enron's fall would break his heart. Trapped in scandal, money lost in heaps, a bitter end, no golden keeps. Greed's lesson learned, a cautionary tale, his name a symbol of corporate fail. His suicide note on January 25, 2002 ,addressed to his wife.

Oh, it's taking rather a long time.

David Goodall, English-born Australian botanist and ecologist. Nature's advocate, explored the world's flora, a green advocate. From the Outback to Amazon's wealth, he sought to understand Earth's stealth. But time caught up, age took its toll, his love for nature, his very soul. A life well-lived, he bid adieu, leaving behind a legacy true on May 10, 2018. He died by assisted suicide at the age of 104.

So the beginning of the eighth day has dawned. It is still cool. I have no water....I am waiting patiently. Come soon please. Fever wracked me last night. Hope you get my full log. Bill.

Bill Lancaster, he flyboy bold, took to the skies, fearless and bold. Across the world, he soared on high, a daring aviator in the sky. But fate had other plans in store, a tragic end forevermore. A life of adventure, now laid to rest, a flying legend, truly the best. He wrote his final note while dying after crash in Sahara Desert in Africa on April 20, 1933.

If I die, do not blame anyone because I am starving. I was making a living by playing piano in a movie theater. Now I can not find this job. You bury me as a Muslim.

Sehzade Ahmed Nuri, a prince so royal and bright, lived a life of luxury, oh, what a sight! With palaces and riches, he was truly blessed, until fate's cruel twist left him laid to rest. An Ottoman prince of high degree, whose life ended in tragic decree. Royals, beware, for fate can be a jest, even for a prince who once was truly blessed. Note found in his pocket after he starved to death in a French public park on August 7, 1944.

To leave this life, to me, is a sweet prospect. When you read this I will be quite dead and no answer will be possible. All I can say is that I offered you love, and the best I could. All I got in return in the end was a kick in the teeth. Thus I die alone and unloved. As you sowed, so shall you reap.

David Ferrie, a pilot so bold and grand, soared through the skies with skills so grand. His flying prowess, oh, so renowned, until his life's journey came crashing down. With mysteries and controversies to his name, his death left many guessing, who was to blame? A tale of aviation, intrigue, and flight, Ferrie's story is shrouded in satirical light. Words written in note (alluding to Galatians 6:7). Ferrie's autopsy concluded that he had died of natural causes on February 22, 1967.

It's too late. We can't win, they've gotten too powerful.

Abbie Hoffman, a radical voice so bold, challenging norms, never consoled. From protests to pranks, he made a scene, a countercultural icon so keen. His wit and satire were his might, but troubles found him day and night. His legacy lives on, a rebel's fight, in the annals of history, shining bright. Words in note written prior to phenobarbital overdose April 12, 1989.

I'm going out for the night. I'll be back—Phil. Love you.

Phil Hartman, a comedic king, with talents that could make hearts sing. From "SNL" to "The Simpsons" fame, his humor brought fortune and acclaim. But tragedy struck, a senseless blow, a life cut short, a bitter woe. His laughter echoes, his loss profound, a legend gone, but never to be forgotten, all around. A note that he had left behind for his wife hours before his murder on May 28, 1998.

It seems that there are no chances. Maybe 10 or 20 percent.

Dmitry Kolesnikov, Russian Navy officer. Fate was cruel, a tragic tale, As his submarine faced a fatal fail. A hero's death, a somber note, A life cut short, a maritime anecdote. Lost at sea, his legacy endures, A submariner's tale, forever lures. Final note written before dying aboard sunken submarine Kursk on August 12, 2000.

Dear Ted, What has happened to us? I don't know. I feel myself in a spiral, going down down down, into a black hole from which there is no escape, no brightness. And loud in my ears from every side I hear, 'failure, failure, failure...' I love you so much ... I am too old and enmeshed in everything you do and are, that I cannot conceive of life without you ... My going will leave quite a rumor but you can say I was overworked and overwrought. Your reputation with your friends and fans will not be harmed ... Sometimes think of the fun we had all thru the years ...

Helen Palmer, a pen-wielding queen, Creating kids' stories was her routine. Editor, author, and philanthropist too, Her stories brought joy to me and you. Her words, a gift to children's lit, Her legacy, still brightly lit. Rest in stories, Helen dear, your tales live on, year after year. Words in her suicide note, addressed to her husband, Theodor Seuss Geisel, on October 23, 1967.

I jumped near the entrance to the dam.

Jonathan Aurthur, wetland warrior bold. His pen a weapon, his cause foretold. Advocating for nature's precious lands, His words like marshes, where wisdom stands. With books and passion, he fought the fight, Rest in peace, champion of wetlands' right. His suicide note was found in his car after he jumped to his death in Angeles National Forest on November 22, 2004.

Probably no one who attempts suicide—is fully aware of all his motives, which are usually too complex. At least in my case it is prompted by a vague sense of anxiety—about my own future. — As for my vague sense of anxiety about my own future, I think I analyzed it all in 'A Fool's Life,' except for a social factor, namely the shadow of feudalism cast over my life. This I omitted purposely, not at all certain that I could really clarify the social context in which I lived. — P.S. Reading a life of Empedocles, I felt how old is this desire to make a God of oneself. This letter, so far as I am conscious, never attempts this. On the contrary, I consider myself one of the most common humans. You may recall those days of twenty years ago when we discussed 'Empedocles on Etna'—under the linden trees. In those days I was one who wished to make a god of myself.

Ry□nosuke Akutagawa, wordsmith supreme. Crafting tales that made readers dream. With wit and satire, he spun his yarns, drawing from life's shadows and life's harms. But, the darkness took its toll, now his stories live on, a literary soul. The final words written in his suicide note on July 24, 1927.

I don't think two people could have been happier than we have been.

Virginia Woolf, a literary queen. Her pen and wit sharp and keen. From Bloomsbury to the River Ouse, she penned words that could amuse. But her own demons, she couldn't tame, her final chapter, a tragic claim. Written to her husband Leonard in her suicide note. Woolf drowned herself later that day on March 28, 1941.

Zweig, the writer with a golden pen. His works cherished by women and men. Tales of love, war, and human plight, captivating readers day and night. But when the darkness of war loomed near, he chose to end it all in fear. Oh, dear! Last words was written in his last testament before committing suicide with his wife, Lotte Altmann, on February 22, 1942.

Thomas Lovell Beddoes, the poet of gloomy themes. Medic by day, scribbler of dark dreams. His pen weaved tales of death and despair, with wit and satire, a macabre affair. But, his own life met a tragic end, a playwright's final, ironic trend. Amen. Last words concluding his suicide note on January 26, 1849.

Lucy Maud Montgomery, a writer so fine. Her tales of Anne, a beloved design. From Prince Edward Island, her stories did spring, a literary sensation, the authorial queen. But life's struggles weighed, her heart forlorn, her final chapter, a tragic mourn. Shorn. Words written on a note found on her bedside table after her death on April 24, 1942.

Robert Benchley, the humor kingpin, quipped with wit, a comedic spin. From essays to films, his humor so bright, brought laughter to all, day and night. But alas, his jests took their toll, his health declined, a heavy toll. With laughter in his final breath, he left the world, chuckling to death. Oh, Benchley, you made us grin, your satire lives on, a comedic win! Final words which he jotted beside the title of an essay which he was reading, "Am I Thinking?" on November 21, 1945.

Depression! Many thanks to all my friends. Many thanks to Professor Felice Lieh-Mak (Cheung's last psychiatrist). This year has been so tough. I can't stand it anymore. Many thanks to Tong Tong (nickname for Cheung's boyfriend Daffy Tong). Many thanks to my family. Many thanks to Sister Fei. In my life I have done nothing bad. Why does it have to be like this?

Leslie Cheung, a star so bright. In music and film, a dazzling sight. From Hong Kong's cinema to global acclaim, his talent and charm, brought fortune and fame. But life's dark shadows, his heart did strain, a final note, a tragic refrain. In vain. His suicide note April 1, 2003. Written before leaping from the 24th floor of the Mandarin Oriental hotel in Hong Kong.

If you or someone you know is in immediate danger of harming themselves, please call your local emergency services or go to your nearest hospital. Suicide hotlines and crisis lines that you can call for help and support: Argentina: +5402234930430, Australia: 13 11 14, Austria: 142, Belgium: 106, Brazil: 188, Canada: 1-833-456-4566, Denmark: +45 70 201 201, Finland: 010 195 202, France: 01 45 39 40 00, Germany: 0800 111 0 111, India: 91-22-27546669, Ireland: 116 123, Italy: 800 86 00 22, Japan: +81 (0) 3 5286 9090, Mexico: 55-5259-8121, Netherlands: 0900-0113, New Zealand: 0800 543 354, Norway: +47 22 40 00 40, Philippines: 2919 or 804-4673, Poland: 116 123, Portugal: 808 200 204, Russia: 007 (8202) 577-577, South Africa: 0861 322 322, South Korea: 1577-0199, Spain: 717 003 717, Sweden: 0771-22 00 60, Switzerland: 143, United Kingdom: 116 123, United States: 1-800-273-8255.

Vain Until The End

All my life I have carried myself gracefully.

Rodrigo Calderón, Count of Oliva on October 21, 1621, when his confessor chastised him for his attention to his appearance prior to his execution by beheading. Being almost 400 years before Tinder, no one else thought it mattered at the time.

Don't cut my face.

Skule Bårdsson, Norwegian nobleman (24 May 1240), before being killed by supporters of King Haakon IV of Norway.

They applauded me!

Louis Philippe II, Duke of Orléans, remembers his former acclaim on the way to the guillotine on November 6, 1793. Some may say the applause was from all his illegitimate children. The Duke, ever the showman, reportedly wore a stylish red waistcoat to his beheading. How fitting, given that he was about to lose his head in the most literal sense. Talk about a fashion statement!

Monsieur de Montaigu, consider what I owe to God, the favor He has shown me, and the great indulgence for which I am beholden to Him. Observe how they are swelled; time to depart.

Anne of Austria, former Queen of France (20 January 1666), looking at her formerly beautiful hands.

Do I look all right? Give me my brush and my makeup.

Ingrid Bergman, a screen siren supreme, graced Hollywood with her talent's gleam. From Casablanca to Notorious, she shined bright, enchanting audiences with her cinematic might. But life's plot took turns, a love scandal unfolded, Ingrid's name was tarnished, yet her legacy remained untarnished. A true legend, forever in our hearts, her star still shines, even after life departs. Final words spoken upon hearing she had a visitor on August 29, 1982.

Soldiers, save my face; aim at my heart. Farewell.

Joachim Murat, the dashing king. His rule, a daring and flashy thing. Napoleon's brother-in-law in command, a throne he claimed with audacious hand. But fate's cruel twist, his reign did cease, condemned to face a firing piece. A royal tale of glory and woe, a monarch's life, a tragic show. Final words on October 13, 1815 to his firing squad.

If this is what viral pneumonia does to one, I really don't think I shall bother to have it again.

Gladys Cooper, a thespian of great renown. From stage to screen, she wore the acting crown. Her legacy, a treasure trove of skill, her performances, a masterclass thrill. Alas, she bid adieu, the final act, but her talent lives on, an eternal fact. She was speaking while looking in a mirror when she said her last words on November 17, 1971.

Wait a second.

Madame de Pompadour, beauty so bright. Chief mistress to Louis, France's king of the night. Her charms and wit, a royal delight. But her power and influence, a courtly fight. Her lavish lifestyle, opulent and grand, bathed in luxury, wealth at her command. Yet envy and jealousy, a venomous brew. Noble snobs sneered, as scandals grew. Her legacy, a patron of arts refined, a taste for fashion, music and design. But her fate was sealed, by illness untamed, even a king's favor, couldn't stop death's claim. She was applying rouge to her cheeks before her death on April 15, 1764.

What an artist dies in me!

Nero, Rome's emperor in the past. A tyrant known to be quite crass. He fiddled while Rome went ablaze. In debauchery, he spent his days. With power corrupt and ego high, his reign ended in a fiery sky. A tale of excess, greed, and vice, a cautionary tale, not nice. Infamous for his cruelty and extravagance, met his end in a fittingly dramatic way. As the Roman Senate declared him an enemy of the state, he reportedly exclaimed, "What an artist dies in me!» as he stabbed himself to death. It's almost as if he were more concerned about his legacy as a performer than as a ruler. But at least he went out with a bang on June 9, 68 CE.

What's that? Do I look strange?

Robert Louis Stevenson, a wordsmith bright. With tales of adventure and eerie fright. From Treasure Island to Jekyll and Hyde, imagination ran wild, no place to hide. His travels wide, his stories grand, a literary genius, across the land. Though his life cut short, his legacy clear, a master storyteller, we still revere. Final words to his wife, Fanny Stevenson, before collapsing from a cerebral hemorrhage on December 3, 1894. He might have looked strange. But he did have great looking hair.

One Last Question

Is it the Fourth?

Thomas Jefferson, a true Renaissance man and one of the great thinkers of American history. Because nothing says "enlightenment" like owning hundreds of slaves and fathering children with one of them. Not so enlightened, he spoke his last words on the third of July. He died on July 4, 1826, the same day as the 50th anniversary of the Declaration of Independence.

Thomas Jefferson survives.

John Adams, the second President of the United States and a true visionary. Because nothing says "achievement" like enacting the Alien and Sedition Acts, which allowed for the arrest and deportation of political dissidents. Adams also made headlines with his dying words, claiming Jefferson survived, unaware that Jefferson had died just hours earlier that same day. Nailing the Fake News, but it took some years before it was trending.

Are we not children, all of us?

Jane Taylor, an English poet, cunningly promoted her poem "Twinkle, Twinkle, Little Star" with her last words before dying on April 13, 1824. Responsible for driving some parents mad when listening to the lullaby on repeat ever since.

I done told you my last request ... a bulletproof vest?

Amerian murderer **James W. Rodgers** last request, spoken when facing a firing squad, was declined one last time on March 31, 1960.

I come, I come, why dost thou call for me?

Zeno of Citium, a Greek philosopher, quoting Aeschylus' play Niobe in 262 BCE, and striking the ground with his hand after sustaining a minor injury, which he considered a sign that he was about to die. He then killed himself.

Why? Why not?

Timothy Leary, a mind explorer. Tripping on psychedelics, a cosmic tour. With "Turn on, tune in, drop out" as his creed, he sought enlightenment, with mind's speed. But society frowned, and laws cracked down, leaving Leary in a legal showdown. A controversial figure, ahead of his time, a psychedelic icon, a visionary climb. In the end, he passed away, but his legacy still shines today. A rebel, a maverick, a psychedelic sage, Timothy Leary, an unforgettable page. Spoken before Leary took his last trip on May 31, 1996.

When will the republic find a citizen like me?

Marcus Livius Drusus, a Roman bold. With political ambitions, he was told. Reforms he sought, for plebeian rights, but the Senate resisted, with all its might. His efforts thwarted, his fate sealed, a political game, a battlefield, a tragic end, a life cut short, In Roman politics, a harsh retort. Last words after being fatally wounded by an assassin 91 BCE.

Where is my clock?

His clock is EVERYWHERE these days, but **Salvador Dalí**, the Spanish surrealist painter, did not find it before dying on January 23, 1989.

Who is it? Who is it?

Knock, knock … **Billy the Kid**, an American outlaw and gunfighter entered a dark bedroom whereupon sheriff Pat Garrett shot him after recognizing his voice on July 14, 1881.

Ah, the cows?

A cow can usually live for around 20 years. Supposedly, the oldest age recorded for a cow was 48 years and 9 months. She was named Big Bertha. Fair warning, it is the Irish that are claiming this. **Erik Satie** was around ten years older than Big Bertha when he died on July 1, 1925.

My God, what's happened?

Princess Diana, a royal tale. With media frenzy, a constant hail. Her charity work, widely praised, but paparazzi's chase, a life ablaze. A tragic end, mourned worldwide, a royal icon, forever tied. To fame and fortune, a tumultuous fate, a princess remembered, never to abate. Last words spoken shortly after being fatally injured in a car accident on August 31, 1997.

Oh, Swaim, this terrible pain. Press your hand on it. Oh, Swaim. Oh, Swaim, can't you stop this?

James A. Garfield, the 20th President of the United States, left behind a legacy as brief as his time in office. He managed to get shot just four months into his presidency. He didn't have any major accomplishments to his name, but at least he had a cool beard until his death on September 19, 1881. He spoke his last words to his friend, General David Swaim.

Must I leave it unfinished?

Adam Naruszewicz, a Polish-Lithuanian bishop and author, was referring to his work "History of the Polish Nation. He died on July 8, 1796, leaving it unfinished.

And where do you come from?

Isaiah Berlin, Russian-British philosopher, speaking before his last breath on November 5, 1997. Making us all philosophizing ever after. What did he see, and where did he/she/it/them/they come from?

I am not mistaken, surely, in believing you to have been formerly my fellow-soldier?

Pompey the Great, how grand was thy fall! From emperor to exiled, the mighty did crawl. Betrayed by his allies, and stabbed in the back, poor Pompey met his end with a mighty thwack. But fear not, dear readers, for though he is dead, in history books and tales, he lives on instead. Dying September 28, 48 BC, he lost all his power. Your agony is gone too, this bad rhyme is over!

You too, my child?

Julius Caesar, the famous Roman general, was killed on March 15, 44 BC, in Rome. He was strutting around like he owned the place, as one does when they're the ruler of an empire. But little did he know, a group of conspirators was plotting against him. They were fed up with his shenanigans and decided to take matters into their own hands. He was stabbed to death by a group of senators led by Marcus Junius Brutus. Others claim his last words was "And you, Brutus?". Rumor has it that Brutus was Caesar's illegitimate son. Talk about a family affair. It's like something straight out of a soap opera. So, there you have it. Julius Caesar met his untimely demise at the hands of his son (allegedly). It's like something Shakespeare would write about...oh wait, he did.

Will no one have pity on me? Here, fire here?

Gabriel de la Concepción Valdés, a Cuban poet pointed at his heart and went with out with a bang during his execution by firing squad on June 26, 1844.

Are the doctors here? Doctor, my lungs...

Benjamin Harrison, the 23rd president of the United States, was known for his forgettable presidency and his forgettable last words. He was so unremarkable that people often mistook him for his grandfather, William Henry Harrison, who served only 32 days in office. It's hard to tell if he accomplished anything during his presidency, but at least he had a nice mustache before he died of pneumonia on March 13, 1901.

What is the answer? In that case, what is the question?

Gertrude Stein, an American writer. With "a rose is a rose is a rose" refrain, Her avant-garde art, hard to explain. A patron of the arts, a salon hostess too, Her legacy lives on, in words anew. Though her death came, her words still thrive, Gertrude Stein, a literary dive. Her final words left her partner Alice B. Toklas questioning before dying on July 27, 1946.

O children, whither are you going?

Cratesiclea, queen of Sparta's reign. A warrior queen, no need to explain. She fought in battles, led with might. Her bravery known, her courage bright. But alas, her end came, a tragic fate, a Spartan queen, forever great, Her legacy lives on, a legendary tale, Cratesiclea, a queen who'll never fail. Final words spoken after seeing the children of her family executed before her execution in 219 BCE.

O my poor soul, whither are you going?

Emperor Hadrian, a ruler wise and fair. With Roman Empire under his care. Built walls and temples, left his mark, a statesman skilled, a ruler stark. His travels vast, his governance great, till death approached, sealed his fate. An emperor renowned, in history's scroll, Hadrian's legacy, a mighty role. Last words before dying from heart failure, at the age of 62, in his villa near Naples on 10 July 138 CE.

Do you have it now?

John Denver, a troubadour of folk. With guitar strums and melodies evoke. His voice so pure, his songs so sweet, From "Country Roads" to "Annie's Song" complete. But a plane crash ended his earthly flight, his music lives on, soaring with delight. John Denver, a legend, still cherished today. In the hearts of fans, forever to stay. He asked if he had transmitted a four-digit code properly before the crash of his experimental Rutan Long-EZ aircraft on October 12, 1997.

God, don't let me die. I have so much to do.

Huey Long, United States Senator after being fatally shot on September 10, 1935. He had travelled to the State Capitol to pass a bill that would gerrymander the district of an opponent. He was killed by his opponents son-in-law juster after passage of the bill.

Are you guys ready? Let's roll.

Todd Beamer, American passenger on United Airlines Flight 93 (11 September 2001), signaling the start of the revolt against the flight's hijackers, resulting in the plane crashing in the ensuing struggle for the controls, killing all 44 aboard, but likely saving countless others.

Should I lift my head a bit?

Dmitry Bogrov, a man with a plan. Assassinated Stolypin, the Russian Prime Minister, a daring fan. With a gun in hand, he took his shot, but his actions brought a web of plots. Caught and condemned, his fate was sealed, a controversial figure in history's field. Spoke his last words to his executioner prior to hanging.

No. What has happened?

Empress Elisabeth of Austria: beautiful, unhappy, assassinated. A reminder that royalty is not always a fairy tale ending. Final words when asked if she was in pain after being stabbed by Italian anarchist Luigi Lucheni on September, 1898.

Nurse, nurse, what murder! What blood! Oh! I have done wrong? God pardon me!

Child king **Charles IX,** ordered deaths. Haunted by sins until last breath. Death at twenty-three, legacy of distress, Tomb brought no peace, only unrest. Last words spoken on May 30, 1574.

Have you brought the chequebook, Alfred?

Samuel Butler, a genius ahead of his time, died in relative obscurity, much like his literary works. Despite his wit and innovation, he struggled to gain recognition in his lifetime, ultimately meeting his end as a modest, unassuming figure. But fear not, dear readers, for his legacy lives on. Now, in this age of social media, it's easier than ever to appreciate the sharp humor and acute observations he made about society over a century ago. Who needs money and fame when your words can live forever on the internet? Rest in peace, Samuel Butler, the ultimate underdog of English literature. Last words before dying on June 18, 1902.

But the peasants...how do the peasants die?

Leo Tolstoy, the ultimate tortured artist. His life was a constant struggle between his literary genius and religious ideals. When he died, his fans mourned the loss of a brilliant mind, while the church celebrated the gain of a devoted follower. It's almost like he wrote his own tragic ending, with characters that echoed his own struggles. But hey, at least we got War and Peace out of it, right? Rest in peace, Leo, your legacy lives on in countless pages and literary analysis essays. Last words spoken to a station master in whose home he died on November 20, 1910.

Why fear death? Death is only a beautiful adventure.

Known for his love of drama, **Charles Frohman** truly lived and breathed the stage. He produced countless hits, from Peter Pan to Sherlock Holmes, and was always looking for his next blockbuster. But alas, fate had other plans for our dear Frohman. In the end, he went down with the Titanic, a tragedy that was almost too perfect for a man who lived for theatrics. Frohman He was paraphrasing Peter Pan prior to dying in the sinking of the RMS Lusitania.

Well, we fooled 'em for a long time, didn't we?

Zip the Pinhead, a man of such exceptional intelligence, was celebrated for his bulbous, pin-sized head. His unique talents were recognized throughout his life and also in death. A man whose brain was so small that it was barely there, yet somehow capable of entertaining millions. His legacy is a testament to the power of being unique, even if it means being reduced to a sideshow attraction. Let us all learn from Zip's life and death, and embrace the freakish aspects of ourselves because who knows, perhaps someday even we could become a beloved oddity. Last words spoken on April 9, 1926.

What is the news?

Clarence W. Barron, the de facto manager of The Wall Street Journal, was a man who knew how to count. He counted words, he counted pages, and he certainly counted profits. Barron's life was a caricature of capitalism, a testament to the power of the almighty dollar. His death, much like his life, was shrouded in wealth and prestige. His legacy will forever be remembered as one surrounded by financial success, and of course, a newspaper or two. Final words spoken on October 2, 1928.

I think I'll go for a drive before dinner – anyone coming?

Brian Oswald Donn-Byrne, the man, the myth, the literary legend. The Irish novelist spoke his final words on June 18, 1928 before dying in auto accident.

How are the lads? Did we do it?

Henry Segrave, British land speed and water speed record pioneer, mortally injured in crash of Miss England II. He was asking his wife about the fates of his chief engineer (who was killed) and his mechanic (who survived), and whether they had broken the water speed record (they had) on June 13, 1930.

Why should I talk to you? I've just been talking to your boss.

Wilson Mizner was a man of many jobs - playwright, entrepreneur, and general mischief-maker. His witty plays were a hit on Broadway, and his shady business deals earned him a reputation as a swindler. He lived life to the fullest, constantly pushing boundaries and creating scandals. Some even claim he was involved in heists and cons, but nothing was ever proven. Sadly, his wild ride came to an end in 1933 when he passed away at the age of 52. Despite the controversy, he left behind a legacy of laughter and a reminder that life is meant to be lived to the fullest. Last words spoken to a priest at his deathbed on April 3, 1933.

Mi madre! Mi madre! Where is my mother? I'm all alone in this country. Don't leave me, Jack.

Alfonso, Prince of Asturias, lived a life of regal splendor, with a silver spoon in his mouth and a golden scepter in his hand. He hobnobbed with dukes and duchesses, while his subjects scraped by on crumbs. But alas, his reign was short-lived, as fate dealt him a fatal blow. Now, he rests in peace, his princely title passed on to the next lucky heir. Oh, the woes of royalty, what a heavy cross to bear! Last words spoken when dying of internal bleeding after car accident in Miami, Florida on September 6, 1938.

Did they get off?

Douglas Albert Munro, United States Coast Guardsman and Medal of Honor recipient, to his friend Raymond Evans after using his Higgins boat to direct fire away from evacuating American troops on September 27, 1942.

Did I get Jimmy out?

Karl Gravell, GC, Royal Canadian Air Force Leading Aircraftman after unsuccessful attempt to rescue Flying Officer James Robinson from wreckage of crashed Tiger Moth on November 10, 1941.

Walter, who knows what is the scheme of things? My suffering has all been for the purpose of making you a man.

Moses Annenberg, the media mogul with ink in his veins, printed headlines that made the world spin. His newspapers told stories with a twist, shaping truth with a flick of his wrist. But scandal struck, his empire crumbled fast, with legal woes and a verdict cast. His final chapter, a cautionary tale, of how power and wealth could easily fail. The press tycoon silenced, his legacy stained, a cautionary tale of the media game. Finals words to his son, Walter Annenberg, on 20 July, 1942. Moses Annenberg had been released from prison a month earlier after being convicted of tax evasion.

Are you all right?

Ernie Pyle, the war reporter extraordinaire, embedded with troops, faced the battlefield glare. His stories vivid, his words profound, capturing war's horrors all around. But alas, his fate was grim and dire, as the bullets flew, his end drew nigher. Now, he rests in peace, a legend revered, his journalistic legacy persevered. War is hell, but Ernie knew, and his satirical take on it was all too true. Last words spoken to Lt. Col. Joseph B. Coolidge before being fatally shot on Iejima during the Battle of Okinawa on April 18, 1945.

Why crying? This is a moment of joy, a moment of glory.

Pope John XXIII, the pontiff maverick, Vatican's rebel, quite the classic. With humor, warmth, and Vatican II, he shook things up, turned the screw. Reforms sparked, traditions bent, but in his coffin, he was sent. A pope ahead of his time, a satirical divine, now resting in heavenly shine. Amen, Pope John, you'll always shine! Speaking to his secretary before dying on June 3, 1963.

What's the time?

It's time to get ill? **Barney Barnato**, a capitalist maverick. Made a fortune in diamonds, slick and quick. Lived large in mansions, wealth galore. But karma struck, death by sea, his riches no more. He asked this question before jumping overboard from a ship on June 14, 1897.

Am I dying or is this my birthday?

Nancy Astor, the bold socialite, the first lady in the House, what a sight! Her wit and charm, a fiery tongue, she ruled the roost, speeches well-sprung. But in her later years, the curtain drew, her final act, the last adieu. A trailblazer, with sass and flair, resting now, in satirical lair. She was awakening on her deathbed to see her entire family around her when she died 17 days before her birthday on May 2, 1964.

Why can't I give up at last?

Buster Keaton, the stone-faced star, performed stunts that pushed the bar. From silent films to slapstick feats, his deadpan gaze, unbeatable treats. But the camera's gaze, it took its toll, as life's struggles took their toll. In the end, he left the screen, a comedic legend, now serene. Rest in slapstick, Buster dear, your satire still brings endless cheer! Last words spoken on February 1, 1966.

Do you know where I can get any shit?

Lenny Bruce, the comic raconteur, pushed boundaries, that's for sure. With jokes so sharp, they cut through norms, his humor challenged social forms. But censors frowned, the law drew near, they silenced him with legal fear. A comic genius, silenced in flight, a satirical voice, gone from the limelight. Rest in laughter, Lenny, old friend, your humor's legacy will never end. Bruce was asking about the availability of drugs before dying on August 3, 1966.

Are you there, Pam? Pam, are you there?

Jim Morrison, the enigmatic poet-king, sang of freedom, let his soul take wing. With rebellious spirit, rock god's grace, he lived life fast, an eternal chase. But alas, his flame burned bright, then dimmed, a rock star's life, the ultimate whim. His legacy lives on, in myth and lore, a poet's soul, forevermore. Spoke his last words to his girlfriend Pamela Courson on July 3, 1971.

Oh God! No! Help! Someone help?

Sal Mineo, the heartthrob of his day, acted with passion, in every way. From Rebel Without a Cause to the stage, he charmed audiences, all the rage. But irony struck, a cruel twist, his life cut short, a fate dismissed. A star extinguished, a talent bright, Sal Mineo, gone into the night. Final words while being murdered on February 12, 1976.

What do you think I'm gonna do? Blow my brains out?

Terry Kath, Chicago's guitar ace, rocked the stage with his fiery embrace. His soulful voice, his shredding riffs, a rock legend, adored by his fans' whiffs. But fate was cruel, a tragic end, a gun mishap, a heartbreaking trend. His talent silenced, a somber chord, Terry Kath, forever adored, yet mourned. Finally words spoken on January 23, 1978 before accidentally shooting himself.

Do you really think the IRA would think me a worthwhile target?

Louis Mountbatten, royal and bold, with titles plenty, and stories told. A naval officer, a statesman wise, with leadership that reached the skies. But irony struck, a tragic blow, a bomb at sea, a merciless foe. His legacy lives on, a life well spent, Lord Mountbatten, a legend, heaven-sent. Spoken prior to death on August 27, 1979 in IRA bombing of his fishing boat.

When I meet God, I am going to ask him two questions: Why relativity? And why turbulence? I really believe he will have an answer for the first.

Werner Heisenberg, a physicist so bright, Uncertainty principle, his intellectual might. Quantum mysteries, equations grand, But caught in a war-torn land. Nazi regime, his country's plight, Did he build the bomb? Oh, what a fright! Debate and speculation, theories abound, Heisenberg's life, a paradox profound. In the end, he passed away, Leaving us puzzled, come what may. A physics genius, a moral haze, Heisenberg's legacy, a quantum maze. Final words before dying on February 1, 1976.

I've got to be crazy to do this shot? I should've asked for a double.

Vic **Morrow**, a talented thespian, with roles aplenty, a rising sensation. On set he shined, with skills renowned, but fate had plans, a twist profound. A helicopter stunt, a tragic flight, a life cut short, a sudden plight. Irony's cruel hand, a somber end, Vic Morrow, remembered, a talent to transcend. Last words before being killed along with two child actors during filming in the Twilight Zone accident on July 23, 1982.

Why? Why?

Rebecca **Schaeffer,** a rising star, on screen and off, she went far. Her talent, beauty, and charm so bright, the future seemed to hold just right. But irony struck, a stalker's hand, a senseless act, a tragedy so grand. Her life cut short, a cruel twist, Rebecca Schaeffer, forever missed. Final words after being shot at her apartment doorsteps by stalker Robert John Bardo on July 18, 1989.

What is this?

Leonard **Bernstein**, maestro supreme, his music's power, a dreamer's theme. From symphonies to West Side Story, his genius soared, in all its glory. But irony played, a satirical prank, as death's baton, cut short his rank. A maestro's legacy, forever alive, Bernstein's melodies, continue to thrive. Spoke his last words on October 14, 1990 when receiving an injection.

Will it be an interesting experience? Will I find out what lies beyond the barrier? Why does it take so long to come?

Graham **Greene**, a literary mind, wrote tales of intrigue, both dark and kind. From Brighton Rock to The Quiet American, his words profound, a novelist's pantheon. But life's irony, a twist of fate, Greene's demise, a mysterious debate. A final chapter, with secrets veiled, Graham Greene's legacy, forever hailed. Final words to his companion Yvonne Cloetta moments before dying on April 3, 1991.

❧

Even A Few Sporty People

No, Bill, I've got too much Georgia grit for that.

Richard Von Albade Gammon, a football star. With speed and skill, he'd go far. On the gridiron, he'd shine bright, Scoring touchdowns left and right. But injuries took their toll, a heavy toll, his career cut short, a bitter blow. Leaving a legacy, a talent lost, a football hero, now a legend crossed. Albade was fatally injured in game on 31, October 1897. He was responding to teammate who asked if he was going to give up.

Are you guys okay?

Thurman Munson, baseball's captain cool, a catcher's prowess, a fielding jewel. With bat in hand, he swung with might, leading the Yankees to championship height. But fate was cruel, a tragic blow, a plane crash took him, too soon to go. A baseball star, now heaven's gain, Thurman Munson, eternally in the Hall of Fame. Trapped in crashed plane, Munson spoke his last words on August 2, 1979, to his two passengers, who survived.

Max **Baer**, the boxing champ, a fierce fighter, with a powerful vamp. He dodged and weaved, threw lethal hooks, left opponents in awe, with puzzled looks. A heavyweight legend, with swagger and flair, but fame can fade, a brutal affair. Baer's final bell, a ring's last tone, a champion's legacy, forever known since dying of a heart attack on November 21, 1959.

How did the Mets do today?

Moe **Berg**, the ballplayer redefined, with brains and brawn, quite a find. From field to field, he roamed with ease, but his true passion was overseas. A spy by trade, a baseball ace, a paradox in time and space. His double life, a tale to tell, a diamond player, a spy as well. Last words spoken to his nurse on May 29, 1972.